Y0-CBA-243

Slingerlands, NY 12159-9295

# FOR GREATER GLORY:
# THE TRUE STORY OF CRISTIADA

## THE CRISTERO WAR AND MEXICO'S
## STRUGGLE FOR RELIGIOUS FREEDOM

# FOR GREATER GLORY:
# THE TRUE STORY OF CRISTIADA

## THE CRISTERO WAR AND MEXICO'S
## STRUGGLE FOR RELIGIOUS FREEDOM

RUBEN QUEZADA

Every reasonable effort has been made to determine copyright holders of excerpted materials and to secure permission as needed. If any copyrighted materials have been inadvertently used in this work without proper credit being given in one form or another, please notify Saint Joseph Communications, Inc., in writing so that future printings of this work may be corrected accordingly.

Published by

**Saint Joseph Communications, Inc.**
*In association with*
**Ignatius Press**

Copyright © 2012 by Saint Joseph Communications, Inc.
Published 2012.

14 13 12 11 10  2 3 4 5 6 7 8 9

All rights reserved.  With the exception of short excerpts for critical reviews, no part of this work may be reproduced or transmitted in any manner or form without permission in writing from the publisher.  Write:

Saint Joseph Communications, Inc.
P.O. Box 720
West Covina. CA 91793

ISBN: 978-1-57058-954-6

Photos from *For Greater Glory* courtesy of ARC Entertainment
Photo credit:  Hana Matsumoto
Historical photos courtesy Museo Cristero
Cover design: John Herreid
Cover Photo: Hana Matsumoto

# DEDICATION

---

*To Father Raymond T. Brannon, S.J. (R.I.P.), who
first introduced me to Blessed Miguel Agustin Pro
and our Mexican martyrs.*

*And especially to Our Lady of Guadalupe in gratitude
for her protection and intercession for all those who stood
up for religious freedom during this struggle.*

A.M.D.G.

# ACKNOWLEDGEMENTS

The author would like to thank the following for making this project a reality:

Archbishop of Los Angeles José H. Gomez, Supreme Knight Carl Anderson, and Eduardo Verástegui, for their generosity and support of this project.

Tony Ryan and Mark Brumley of Ignatius Press, for reaching out to me for this very special project and for their great leadership.

Lisa Wheeler and all at The Maximus Group, for their vision and commitment to make this happen in such a short period of time.

Terry Barber, President of St. Joseph Communications, for allowing me to take the time necessary from my other commitments to make this happen.

Project Manager and Editor Matthew Arnold, for his unending support, vision, and valuable time to make this book a reality.

# TABLE OF CONTENTS

# FOREWORD

The anti-Catholic persecutions in Mexico in the 1920s and 1930s are long forgotten, it seems.

The reality is hard to believe. Just a generation ago, not far from our borders, thousands of men, women and even children, were imprisoned, exiled, tortured, and murdered. All for the "crime" of believing in Jesus Christ and wanting to live by their faith in him.

So I welcome the new film, *For Greater Glory*. It tells the dramatic story of this unknown war against religion and our Church's heroic resistance. It's a strong film with a timely message. It reminds us that our religious liberties are won by blood and we can never take them for granted.

That such repression could happen in a nation so deeply Catholic as Mexico should make everybody stop and think. Mexico was the original cradle of Christianity in the New World. It was the missionary base from which most of North and South America, and parts of Asia, were first evangelized.

Yet following the revolution in 1917, the new atheist-socialist regime vowed to free the people from all "fanaticism and prejudices."

Churches, seminaries and convents were seized, desecrated and many were destroyed. Public displays of piety and devotion were outlawed. Catholic schools and newspapers were shut down; Catholic political parties and labor unions banned. Priests were tortured and killed, many of them shot while celebrating Mass.

The dictator, Plutarco Elías Calles, used to boast about the numbers of priests he had executed. His hatred of organized religion ran deep. He really believed his reign of terror could exterminate the Church and wipe the memory of Christ from Mexico within a single generation.

He was wrong. In the forge of his persecution, saints were made.

It became a time of international Catholic solidarity. American Catholics opened their doors to refugees fleeing the violence. My predecessor, Archbishop John J. Cantwell, welcomed many here to Los Angeles — including Venerable Maria Luisa Josefa de la Peña and Blessed María Inés Teresa Arias.

Ordinary Catholics became *Cristeros*, courageous defenders of Jesus Christ. Many felt compelled to take up arms to defend their rights in what became known as the Cristero War. Others chose nonviolent means to bear witness to Christ.

"I die, but God does not die," Blessed Anacleto González Flores said before his execution. His words were prophetic.

Martyrs are not defined by their dying but by what they choose to live for. And the Cristeros' blood became the seed for the Church of future generations in Mexico.

I hope *For Greater Glory*, and this little companion book, will bring more people to know the stories of the Cristeros martyrs.

We need to know about the beautiful young catechist, Venerable María de la Luz Camacho. When the army came to burn her church down, she stood in front of the door and blocked their way. They shot her dead. But the church was somehow spared.

We need to know about all the heroic priests who risked their lives to celebrate Mass and hear confessions. Growing up, we had prayer cards made from a grainy photograph of one of these priests, Blessed Miguel Pro. He is standing before a firing squad without a blindfold, his arms stretched wide like Jesus on the cross as he cries out his last words: *"¡Viva Cristo Rey!* (Long live Christ the King!")

We need to learn from the examples of all the Cristeros who have been canonized and beatified by the Church. And today especially, we need to pray for their intercession.

As it always has been, today our Catholic religion is under attack in places all over the world. In Mexico and America, we don't face suffering and death for practicing our faith. But we do confront "softer" forms of secularist bullying. And our societies are growing more aggressively secularized.

Already, sadly, we've accepted the "rules" and restrictions of our secular society. We keep our faith to ourselves. We're cautious about "imposing" our beliefs on others — especially when it comes to politics. In recent months, our government has started demanding even more — trying to coerce our consciences—so that we deny our religious identity and values.

We need to ask for the strength to be Cristeros. By their dying, they show us what we should be living for. We need to make that our prayer. That like the Cristeros, we might be always ready to love and sacrifice to stand up for Jesus and his Church.

And may Our Lady of Guadalupe, Mother of Mexico and the Americas, and the bright star of the New Evangelization, pray for us.

The Most Rev. José H. Gomez
Archbishop of Los Angeles
*Memorial of St. Christopher Magallanes, Priest and Companions, Martyrs*
May 21, 2012

# AUTHOR'S PREFACE

I first heard the term "religious persecution" in 1978 when I was a 12-year-old dishwasher at Manresa Jesuit Retreat House in Azusa, California. The director, Fr. Raymond Brannon, S.J., was the first to introduce me to this expression. Although elderly, he would sit behind the large desk in his private residence where he still did his own administrative work. Oftentimes he would eat his meals there and I would come in to pick up the dishes.

One day as we spoke, I noticed a small prayer card taped to the wall behind him. It was a bit old and had turned yellow from the smoke of his ever-present cigarettes. "Who is he?" I asked, pointing to the card. Father turned around and, after searching his note-filled wall, realized to whom I was referring. He said, "Fr. Pro! He's Mexican, like you. Don't you know about him?" I shrugged my shoulders and shook my head. Father continued, "He was killed in Mexico for being a priest." Then, to my surprise, he raised his arms and made a gesture of someone firing a rifle and exclaimed, "Boom! That's what Mexico was doing with their priests. And one of them was one of ours, a Jesuit."

"No way," I thought, "that's impossible."

He took the card from the wall, stretched out his hand, and laid it onto mine saying, "Here, you can have it. Learn about him and the persecution Mexico waged on Catholics and us priests." I took the card, flipped it over, and read:

Blessed Miguel Agustin Pro, S.J., martyred for the faith on November 23, 1927. Mexico City.

As I was leaving the room, I turned around to see Father one last time, hoping he would let me in on the prank I thought he was pulling. But when I caught his glance before the door closed, he made the same gesture of a soldier firing his weapon. It was true!

I began searching, but found nothing at my local library. However, I was determined to find out more. I would travel often across the border into Mexico and ask my childhood friends if I could see their history books. They were puzzled why I would make such a request. I would tell them I just wanted to reminisce about my childhood years in school. Although I looked thoroughly through each book they offered, I found nothing.

I would often think to myself, "Father was probably joking after all. He just wanted to drive me nuts 'looking for a black cat in a dark room.' He must be laughing his head off." But then reason would always bring me back to the same conclusion: Why would anyone print a prayer card with the story of this executed priest as a prank?

Finally, one of the Jesuit priests at Manresa showed me a book titled *No Strangers to Violence, No Strangers to Love.* It told the story of Blessed Miguel Pro and included the first photographic images of his execution I had ever seen. It had to be true.

In the early 1990s the internet began to open up greater search capabilities and things started popping up about this mysterious priest. I finally located a book about his life story by the late author Ann Ball called *Blessed Miguel Pro*. Needless to say, I was incredibly excited. When it finally arrived I sat down and read it in a single sitting. It took me less than an hour to devour the entire book. I couldn't believe it—much less understand it—this "religious persecution." Later on that night I read it again. Many questions began to pop up and I wanted to find the answers. Why was this peaceful, joyful, and funny priest executed? Isn't Mexico a Catholic country? What did he do to deserve execution? Why didn't anybody stop it?

And so began a journey that would take me both physically and very much emotionally to various parts of the world seeking books, testimonies, pieces of history, and—most importantly—the real truth behind the untimely death of this innocent man of God. When I was finally able to ascertain the truth, it shocked me like nothing I could have ever imagined.

It is truly unimaginable to think that less than a century ago the Catholic Church in Mexico experienced one of the fiercest religious persecutions Latin America has ever seen. This religious persecution occurred during the presidency of Plutarco Elías Calles (1924—1930). His government's effort to eradicate Catholicism from Mexico sent thousands of the faithful onto the battlefield for the sake of religious freedom. The ensuing three-year war became known as La Cristiada. To the cry of "¡Viva Cristo Rey! (Long Live Christ the King!)" many of our priests and lay men were honored with the crown of martyrdom. It was a time when the faithful became outlaws, and priests were executed for celebrating the sacraments of our Catholic Faith, fundamental freedom we possess but seldom appreciate.

Although twenty-five of those killed have been canonized in the past few years, and fifteen others have been beatified with triumphant ceremonies, there are still many more on the path to Sainthood. Of course, we will never know all the true stories of the thousands of courageous men and women who gave the ultimate sacrifice to ensure the religious freedom of generations to come. Most survivors of this persecution have passed away, their stories in danger of becoming only a vague memory.

When I travel the country giving lectures on this topic, many react with shock and disbelief, or simply cannot fathom how a country like Mexico would allow this to happen. Why are so many people, especially those of Mexican heritage, completely oblivious to this part of history? The reason is that the Mexican government made every effort to erase this story—this embarrassment—from its history books and from the minds of its people. And it has done a very good job.

Typical questions that arise during my lectures are: How could this happen in a Catholic country? Why would the Mexican government do such a thing? What were Catholics doing during this time? What happened to the priests? Did the United States help in any way? What did the Vatican do to assist these persecuted Catholics? How long did the persecution last? These questions and many more need to be answered for Catholics and others to understand the importance of this crucial piece of our history.

Luis Rivero del Val was a young Cristero fighter. In his diary/book, *Entre Las Patas de Los Caballos* (*Among the Horses' Hooves*) he writes:

*"[D]ays will come when a future generation will be able to share the names and stories of their true heroes. By then, the chains will be broken and Mexico will learn to appreciate the sacrifice."*

After the truce was signed between the government and the Catholic Church, Luis and the other Cristeros were promised leniency, but were later hunted down and killed.

Every Catholic throughout the world, regardless of national heritage, must learn about the persecution the Church has endured throughout her history. We must take courage from the examples of sacrifice to stand firm and fight for our religious liberty. True freedom is the God-given right to be allowed to do what one ought to do. No merely human agency is entitled to take this away.

This is the theme of the major motion picture *For Greater Glory: The True Story of Cristiada*. I was honored to be asked to write this little book to answer some of the many questions the movie will inspire. And to provide various historical details not included in the film.

I close this brief introduction with what may be the most important question of all. At over one hundred fifty lectures I have given on this topic, almost without fail, someone asks, "Can this persecution happen again?"

You can bet your life on it.

The time to stand up for our religious freedom is now. ¡Viva Cristo Rey!

Ruben Quezada
Covina, California
2012

*Photo Credit: Eva Muntean*

*For Greater Glory* Director Dean Wright (left) with the Author

# INTRODUCTION

Appearing in *For Greater Glory: The True Story of Cristiada* was a remarkable experience for me both as an actor and as a Catholic. I was very blessed to join such an elite international cast for this very special film. It was truly a learning experience and a great blessing to me in more ways than I can explain.

As I learned about Blessed Anacleto González Flores, the character I would portray in the film, I knew I had to try to represent on screen everything he stood for in life. As it turned out, I ended up getting far more from his life story than I could ever give on film.

Anacleto was a man completely submitted to God's will and dedicated to serving His Church. He was a teacher, a lawyer, and a great leader among his peers. He came to be known as the "Mexican Ghandi" since he always fought violence and persecution with peaceful means.

But what truly elevated my gratitude for this blessed martyr, and helped me especially to grow personally, was the example he set when he was executed. He was willing to sacrifice for something greater than himself and was not afraid to give his life. That spoke a million words to me, but I can easily describe him in one word – integrity! His passion, dedication, and commitment to serve God with honor and respect are qualities that all Catholic men and women should be wearing on their sleeves today.

I would also like to thank my good friend and brother in Christ Ruben Quezada for his gracious assistance in helping me learn so much about Anacleto, for his continued support of great causes—such as writing this book—and for his everlasting love for the story of La Cristiada which he has been sharing with others for many years.

I am thrilled to see a book of this type become available so everyone can have a deeper understanding of the authentic history behind the terrible persecution portrayed in *For Greater Glory: The True Story of Cristiada*. I sincerely pray such persecution will never be repeated. I am also very excited to add these words to those contributed to this book by distinguished Catholic leaders Archbishop José H. Gomez of the Archdiocese of Los Angeles and Carl Anderson, Supreme Knight of the Knights of Columbus.

Lastly, I pray for every Catholic today, and for generations to come, that after watching the film and reading this book, they will embrace the same courage and dedication to the principle of religious freedom that our ancestors displayed amidst unspeakable trial and adversity. May the sacrifices of our martyrs of generations past be truly appreciated today, more than ever.

Eduardo Verástegui
Hollywood, California
2012

# QUESTIONS AND ANSWERS

---

# ONE—ORIGINS OF THE CRISTIADA

## Who were the Cristeros?

The Cristeros were men (both Catholic and non-Catholic) who joined together to fight for religious freedom during a persecution of the Catholic Church by the Mexican government in the 1920s.

## Why were they called Cristeros?

Their battle cry was "¡Viva Cristo Rey!" On the battlefront, government forces, or "Federales" heard their battle cry and began referring to them as "Cristos Reyes (Christ Kings)." The words were combined to form the name Cristeros. The Federales used this term as a way to mock or ridicule the Catholic insurgents for their religious beliefs, but to the Cristeros it became a badge of honor.

## What is "¡Viva Cristo Rey!" in English

"¡Viva Cristo Rey!" means "Long Live Christ the King!" This was originally part of a longer motto: "Long Live Christ the King and Long Live Our Lady of Guadalupe!"

As portrayed in the film, the ejaculation "¡Viva Cristo Rey!" was answered with the words, "¡Que viva! (He lives!)." The Calles regime declared that the cry "¡Viva Cristo Rey!" was more than a statement of faith; it was an act of treason.

**How did the Cristeros choose this battle cry?**

First, the devotion to Our Lady of Guadalupe runs deep in the heart of all Catholics in Mexico. In addition, Mexico had been consecrated to Christ the King by Pope Saint Pius X a few years before the persecution; hence, the Cristero's desire to go into battle giving honor to Jesus Christ the King and to His Holy Mother under her title of Our Lady of Guadalupe.

**What was the Cristiada?**

The Cristiada was the name given to the Cristero uprising. The movement was called the "Cristiada" after the Cristeros.

**How did the Cristiada come about and how was it organized?**

The Cristiada was a response to a direct attack on the Catholic faith by President Plutarco Elías Calles. His strict enforcement of the anticlerical provisions of the 1917 Mexican Constitution became known as the "Calles Law."

The Cristero movement was organized by the National League for the Defense of Religious Liberty or Liga Nacional Defensora de la Libertad Religiosa (LNDLR). The LNDLR was a religious civil rights group established in 1925.

Together with the Catholic hierarchy, the League initially advocated peaceful resistance to the Calles Law in the form of boycotting taxes and nonessential goods, and organizing petition drives to rescind the offending constitutional provisions. When the Vatican failed to obtain a compromise from Calles, the Mexican hierarchy ordered the priests to suspend religious services beginning July 31, 1926, the day the Calles Law was to go into effect.

After the clerical suspension, sporadic popular uprisings began to take place, especially in Jalisco and Colima. In 1927 the League reorganized resistance efforts under a military leader, General Enrique Gorostieta.

## When did the Cristiada take place?

The Cristiada, also known as the Cristero War, took place from 1926 to 1929. After a period of peaceful resistance, it became inevitable that Catholics would have to fight back or surrender their religious freedom.

The persecution began on August 1, 1926, when the Mexican government forced the closure of all Catholic churches throughout the entire country according to the Calles Law. The military's persecution of clergy and lay people sparked sporadic armed resistance. However, the first coordinated uprising did not occur until January 1, 1927.

The conflict continued until June 23, 1929, when a truce was signed by representatives of the Catholic Church and the Mexican government, bringing an official end to the Cristero War. The Mexican bishops ordered the LNDLR to cease military and political activities and the Cristeros to lay down their weapons.

## What caused the Mexican Government to persecute ruthlessly the Catholic Church in the first place?

When President Plutarco Elías Calles came into power, he envisioned Mexico as a Socialist utopia in the making. He insisted that the Catholic Church was poisoning the minds of the people and that its moral teachings were a threat to the Revolutionary mentality for which he stood. Like the fervent atheists of today, he did not want God to be a part of anyone's life.

The first two presidents after the Mexican Revolution (Venustiano Carranza and Álvaro Obregon) had likewise abused their power to wage personal attacks against the Catholic Church. There were incidents of persecution and abuses towards clergy and lay Catholics alike, similar to those that would emerge so dramatically under Calles. In fact, there are Mexican martyrs from those post-revolution persecutions that predate the Cristero War.

## Did only Catholics fight in the Cristiada?

Not all who joined the Cristero movement were Catholics and not all Catholics joined the uprising. As happens in every society, some do not take their faith as seriously as others.

While the majority of Cristeros fought for religious freedom, some joined the uprising simply for the love of fighting. Others, bitter over being ousted or defeated during the Mexican Revolution, fought the government for revenge.

Thousands of Catholic citizens supported the Cristiada by joining the uprising. Many others assisted by raising funds, distributing flyers, collecting food and first aid supplies, etc. There was a large movement of support among local leaders, Catholic groups (such as the Knights of Columbus), and private citizens.

Many atrocities were committed by government soldiers. Some of these Federales shared the government's anti-Catholicism or fought for personal interest. Many more were coerced into supporting the government's draconian policies against their own principles and beliefs.

There are many accounts of Federales changing sides to join the Cristeros during the actual fighting. In the crucible of battle, they knew in conscience for which side they had to fight.

**Why did the Cristeros rise up against the Calles regime?**

During this time, the faith of simple Catholics ran deep in Mexico. Mexican lay Catholics had a true passion for their faith back then and it was an important part of their daily lives. They considered it a spiritual necessity to go to Holy Mass and receive the Sacraments.

Before the anticlerical Calles Law took effect in 1926, members of the clergy, Catholic groups (such as the Knights of Columbus), and even some politicians risked arrest in an effort to persuade Congress to rescind this attack on religious freedom. Time after time they were denied.

President Calles wanted to ensure that all citizens would be educated under the totalitarian government's secular standards. He wanted the government to form the minds of Mexico's citizens unopposed and insisted that the Church was "poisoning the minds of the people."

## Of what did the "Calles Law" consist?

In June 1926, Plutarco Elías Calles signed the "Law for Reforming the Penal Code," which became known unofficially as the "Calles Law." The Calles Law's reform of the penal code in Mexico called for the strict enforcement of restrictions against clerics and the Catholic Church that were provisions of the Mexican Constitution of 1917. Some examples of the Constitutional Articles:

Article Three mandated compulsory secular education "free of any religious orientation."

Article Twenty-four concerned "religious freedom" understood as "freedom of worship" so long as it "does not constitute a crime." In other words, there was only as much "freedom of worship" as the government chose to allow. Also, religious institutions were forbidden to own any land beyond their "temples" and even these were subject to confiscation by the state.

Article 130 obliged all churches and religious groups to register with the state. Priests and ministers of all religions were made second-class citizens forbidden to vote, hold public office, support any political party or its candidates, or even criticize public officials.

President Calles not only enforced these existing laws regarding the "separation of church and state" throughout Mexico, but also added his own legislation. The new law imposed specific penalties for priests and individuals who violated the constitutional provisions. Priests would suffer harsh fines for such "offenses" as wearing clerical garb in public or draw five years in prison for so much as simply criticizing the government.

The legislation also decreed that parish priests register with the government and that the churches be placed under control of "neighborhood committees." Obviously, this was not a matter of "separation of church and state," but complete subordination of the Church to the state.

To help enforce the law, Calles seized Church property, expelled all foreign-born priests, and closed the monasteries, convents, and religious schools. Priests and lay people who did not comply were often executed.

**What was the origin of the 1917 Mexican Constitution?**

The Mexican Constitution of 1917 was drafted by a constitutional convention in Santiago de Querétaro during the Mexican Revolution. It was approved by the Constitutional Congress on February 5, 1917. This new Constitution is successor to the Constitution of 1857 and earlier Mexican constitutions.

Articles 3, 5, 24, 27, and 130 were redacted with sections to restrict the influence of the Catholic Church. In April 1917, Mexican bishops prepared a letter of protest that declared the new Constitution "destroys the most sacred rights of the Catholic Church, of Mexican Society, and of Christian individuals." It was the effort by the Calles regime to enforce these articles strictly that led to the uprising known as the Cristiada or Cristero War.

**Who was Plutarco Elías Calles?**

Plutarco Elías Calles was a Mexican general and politician. He was president of Mexico from 1924 to 1928, but he continued to control the political direction of Mexico from 1928–1935. This period is known as the "maximato"— when Calles proclaimed himself "Máximo" or "Jefe Supremo"—which is translated "Supreme Chief."

Calles is most noted for the fierce oppression of Catholics which led to the Cristero War, and for founding the Partido Nacional Revolucionario (National Revolutionary Party, or PNR), which eventually became the Partido Revolucionario Institucional (Institutional Revolutionary Party, or PRI)—which governed Mexico for more than 70 years.

## What was Calles' aim in attacking the Church?

Calles wanted to eradicate Catholicism and create a new Socialist society without God. By doing so, he would gain better control of the people's way of thinking and their way of living.

He would often read books and articles by authors whose writings envisioned a Socialist utopia and he wanted the same for Mexico. It was through this vision that Calles decided to keep the United States and European governments from owning any Mexican oil interest. He wanted Mexico in complete control of its people and its land.

Years later, with no end to Calles' war against the Catholic Church in sight, the U.S. took the opportunity to become a peacemaker—while simultaneously recovering their former lucrative Mexican oil interests.

## How does Calles' personal background relate to his persecution of the Church?

It is important to know that Plutarco Elías Calles grew up in poverty and deprivation. He was the illegitimate son of an alcoholic father who did not provide the necessary means for his family and would eventually abandon them. Plutarco's mother, Maria de Jesús Campuzano, passed away when he was only two years old. He was then raised by his uncle Juan Bautista Calles, from whom he took his surname. A fervent atheist, Juan Bautista instilled in his nephew a fanatical hatred of the Catholic Church.

As an adult, Calles became a general of the Mexican Revolution. Once he became active in politics, he rapidly rose through the ranks to become governor of the state of Sonora before setting his sights on a presidential bid. Once elected president in 1924, he was ready to reform Mexico according to his own uncompromisingly atheist/socialist image through the strict enforcement of the anticlerical provisions of the 1917 Mexican Constitution.

**Did anyone else support this persecution of Catholics?**

Many politicians throughout the country supported the persecution of the Church, while quite a number of citizens also supported the oppression, mostly due to their own atheist beliefs or simple anti-Catholic sentiment.

**How was the Calles Law received by the public?**

As far as the secular citizens were concerned, it was "much ado about nothing." Christian citizens however, especially faithful Catholics, did not receive it well at all.

When religious freedom is forcibly taken from the citizens of any country, there is bound to be resistance, even bloodshed. The bishops of Mexico were the first to respond, followed by the Holy See—doing all it could within its power—plus thousands of citizens who rallied for this law to be lifted.

## TWO – THE CATHOLIC RESPONSE

### Why did the Church suspend religious services?

Catholic priests are obligated to celebrate Holy Mass daily and to celebrate the other Sacraments according to the rules of the Church and the needs of the people. Once the Calles Law went into effect, such public celebrations would be illegal and the penalties fierce. By suspending services, the hierarchy released the priests of their religious obligations and allowed them to comply with the law.

In the film we see Catholic marriages, baptisms, etc. celebrated en masse in anticipation of the enactment of the new law. Also depicted are scenes of the Federales disrupting private services—killing lay people and executing priests. It was such actions that led to the Cristiada.

### What happened to Religious Education during the Cristiada?

All public catechism classes ceased during the persecution for fear of the risk of fines or jail for the participants. Many Catholics continued to teach classes but always in hiding, observing strict secrecy, and with very limited resources. Many of the Catholic schools lost their teaching materials when the government seized all Church properties.

Many marriage licenses, baptismal certificates and other documents dated during this time are merely simple slips of paper , each with the vows, the name of the city, and the priest who celebrated the Sacrament (many of these priests are now considered martyrs) — these simple documents are true gems of the Catholic Faith!

## How many priests or religious were evicted from Mexico?

To enforce the new law better, the government expelled all foreign-born (missionary) Catholic clergy and religious from Mexico. Many seminarians were also exiled. There were 4,500 Mexican priests serving their people before the persecution began in 1926. By 1934 over ninety percent of them suffered persecution. A mere 334 priests were licensed by the government to serve fifteen million people. This led to entire states of Mexico going without a single Holy Mass being celebrated for weeks or months at a time. Over 4,100 Mexican priests were eliminated by emigration, expulsion, or assassination. By 1935, seventeen Mexican states were left with no priests at all.

One can only imagine the feeling of desperation on the part of faithful lay Catholics. Testimony from survivors of the Cristero movement reveals that they would rather go without food than go without assisting at Holy Mass. It was inevitable that this attack on their religious freedom would not be allowed to pass peacefully.

**So Catholics continued to practice their Faith?**

Yes, but only at great risk. During the fiercest parts of the persecution, the government continued to multiply the penalties for Catholics caught in any religious celebration. To be caught in a catholic gathering, a wedding, private Mass, etc., was to be arrested, fined heavily, or even be executed. Fear would discourage thousands of people from practicing their Faith.

The bail for those arrested would be set so high they might lose everything they possessed to pay it. Others were sent to a prison called Islas Marias (Mary Islands) in the Pacific Ocean as punishment. It was a place that no one would ever want to visit—where the Mexican government imprisoned the worst criminals. Catholics young and old were sent there to intimidate others to cease practicing their faith.

Worst of all, anyone caught celebrating any religious services could be summarily executed. Many Catholic clergy were killed by firing squads.

**Were boycotts organized during this time? How were they an effective means to fight back?**

Boycotts are one way to resist the aggressor peacefully. Because Catholics knew that the Church would not support an armed revolt, many opted for peaceful measures to resist the injustice while remaining in full union with the Church.

Many business owners who supported the government were targeted for boycotts. Transportation services were avoided and people kept expenses to an absolute minimum in order to give a financial blow to the economy. Many stores and entertainment facilities, such as theaters, had to close due to this boycott.

## Had the Catholic Church always been under attack in Mexico?

Religious persecution permeates Mexico's history since the deaths of Fr. Miguel Hidalgo and, later, Fr. José Maria Morelos, who had participated in Mexico's War of Independence (1810—1821).

There was religious persecution in the 1870s similar to that of the 1920s Cristero War. During that time the Catholic resistance was called Los Religioneros, or, "The Religioneers" (1873—1876). There was also persecution to a certain extent during the Mexican Revolution (1910—1917) and, most notably, during the Cristero War (1926—1929). Further persecution led to a small resurgence of the Cristiada during the 1930s but did not become as fierce or as widespread as its predecessor.

Even to the present day, the Church in Mexico has labored under continued persecution. The Catholic Church has suffered extensively in our modern era from various anti-Catholic aggressors employing ever more sophisticated means to accomplish their goal of suppressing religious liberty.

## Did Mexican Catholics follow the Calles regime's order to close all Churches?

During the persecution begun in 1926, there were citizens in some areas who were not willing to follow Calles' executive order to close all the churches. When the military would visit such locations to enforce the new law, soldiers would destroy all religious images. They would also use the churches as stables, cockfighting arenas, and for profane social gatherings designed to offend even the most mild-mannered Catholic.

It is hardly surprising that Catholics would fight back to defend their priest and their parish. While these sporadic confrontations were not planned or premeditated, it soon became evident that military persecution was creating an "atmosphere" of valor and courage. Catholics would fight for their religious freedom and the conviction that no one had the right to take it away.

## Was there any active "Catholic" Church in Mexico during this period?

Once the persecution began in earnest, there were very few Catholic priests left in Mexico. During this period the government established the schismatic "Mexican Apostolic Catholic Church" to serve the Catholic community as it would see fit. The government made use of a retired dissident priest, Fr. José Joaquin Perez, as the leader of this state-run "church."

The Mexican Apostolic Catholic Church had no jurisdiction from Rome, refused to recognize the Pope, opposed priestly celibacy (among other teachings of the Church), and charged the faithful for the Sacraments (the sin of simony). Calles' "church" soon closed its doors due to lack of interest from the faithful.

## Who coordinated the first uprising?

The National League for the Defense of Religious Liberty, or Liga Nacional Defensora de la Libertad Religiosa (est. 1925), was the first to fight back, along with local residents who had grown tired of the oppression. They realized that using peaceful means to rescind the new law was a futile effort.

Everyone was desperate to regain religious freedom and return to the sacraments. And the confrontations were simply inevitable in the eyes of many Catholics.

## When did the first uprising take place?

To pinpoint the exact date of the first uprising during this time is difficult because defense against government persecution happened sporadically throughout Mexico and went mostly unreported. The first official uprising is considered to have taken place on January 1, 1927.

The National League for the Defense of Religious Liberty, after months of unsuccessful attempts to rescind the Calles Law, recruited a large number of ex-military veterans who had fought during the Mexican Revolution in a region called Los Altos in the state of Jalisco to coordinate the "first" surprise attack of government forces.

It is significant to point out that, from the beginning, the Cristeros did not have adequate military resources. They could only rely on old weapons, an insufficient supply of ammunition, a few horses, plus hope and prayer.

When the surprise attack was being planned, it was difficult for the Cristeros to foresee a victory. Besides a general skepticism, they had little confidence in their meager forces since the government could count on full military support at the drop of a hat. They knew President Calles would not hesitate to array his military superiority against them.

To the astonishment of all, the surprise attack on January 1, 1927, was a victory for the Cristeros! Although they did lose a few men during this confrontation, their military success was just the spark they needed to fan the flames of courage in defense of the Faith.

### What happened after the first Cristero victory?

As one Cristero wrote in his memoirs:

*"It was unbelievable. They sent these young soldiers so wet behind the ears we felt we had gone cadet hunting. They couldn't mount a horse correctly, they couldn't shoot straight while riding, and some of the young cadets even fell off their horses during the attacks. It was a real shame, but it was either them or us."*

When the last government soldier fell after that first attack, the Cristeros had gained weapons, ammunition, and horses—as well as a new confidence—for their small army. Additional men joined their cause and the Cristeros grew stronger. With this new growth, they were able to plan their defense of the neighboring towns of Los Altos. This is considered the real beginning of the Cristero movement.

### Did the uprising grow?

Although the first uprising was not considered a serious threat to the government, it began spreading like wildfire and engulfed almost the entire country in the three years of fighting. The government failed to see the real threat when the first uprising occurred, which led to this monumental battle throughout Mexico.

One of the Mexican generals who experienced firsthand the attack and defeat of government forces visited President Calles and personally recounted what had occurred. He declared that, if Calles would give him authority to take any military action he deemed necessary, he would have no trouble squashing the insurgents in three weeks.

President Calles responded, "Use whatever means you need to use to eradicate these religious fanatics, so long as it does not take three years!" Ironically, it was three years before the end of the conflict.

## Was there anyone in Mexico who spoke up and came to the aid of the Church?

Besides the thousands on the battlefield fighting for religious freedom, there were thousands of others in local cities who assisted as volunteers; donated money, food, or clothing to relieve suffering; and worked towards the abolition of the Calles Law.

Many citizens lost everything they possessed by showing support for the Cristero cause. Anyone found aiding the Cristeros would be arrested without question.

After the persecution intensified, neighboring countries called on the Mexican government to rescind the law or to end the persecution of religious freedom. Political pressure mounted after the first images of the persecution came to light.

## What is the origin of the existing photos of the Cristeros' executions?

President Calles wanted to ensure that all Catholics would see the horror of the brutal executions in order to intimidate them and to deter them further from practicing their Faith. After the first images were published, the public's response was one of shock, disbelief, and anger. Exposing the horrific measures of the persecution only enraged the people even more and led more of them to support the rebellion. Clearly, Calles had made a huge mistake.

## Who funded the Cristero uprising?

The uprising was funded by local Catholics and grass roots fundraising to obtain cash, guns, ammunition, first aid, food, horses, etc. Thousands of Catholics donated anything and everything they possessed in order to support the cause.

## Who coordinated these fundraisers?

There were many groups involved in order to help the Cristero movement. However, one of the biggest contributors to the cause was the Feminine Brigades of Saint Joan of Arc, or Las Brigadas Femeninas de Santa Juana de Arco.

## Who were the Feminine Brigades of Saint Joan of Arc?

The character of "Adriana," portrayed in *For Greater Glory* by Catalina Sandino Moreno, is representative of the young women who formed the Feminine Brigades of Saint

Joan of Arc. The courageous acts depicted in the film are based on true events.

It was started on June 21, 1927, by a small group of young Catholic women in Jalisco who were sympathetic to the Cristero movement. Although there were fewer than twenty women present at their first meeting, they eventually grew to over 25,000 members in three years.

Their "squadrons" filled many important roles crucial for the survival of the cause. They were organized as communication cells, fundraisers, and nurses. Some of them carried ammunition hidden under their clothing, concealed weapons for the Cristeros, and gave first aid assistance to wounded soldiers. Some lost their lives to exploding grenades during their smuggling operations.

Many more were arrested, raped by their captors, and executed for carrying secret messages aimed to assist the Cristero units. In one incident a general for the government forces had five of these brave young women hung simply for printing antigovernment propaganda. They were considered traitors by their own government, but martyrs for the Cristero cause.

Part of this powerful and important movement to help the Church was a vow of secrecy among the young women. Anyone who was arrested by the local authorities would give no details nor relinquish any information regarding for whom they worked. It was a true hidden movement within the persecution that didn't come to light until near the end in 1929. As Fr. José Reyes Vega (portrayed by Santiago Cabrera) says in *For Greater Glory*, "Without these women, we would be lost."

**Who founded this group of young women?**

The foundress, Mrs. Uribe (also known as Mrs. G. Richaud), held the first meeting in order to propose an organization that would coordinate every possible effort to assist the Cristeros on the battlefield without actually engaging in battle. Most were young, educated, single Catholic women who were willing to give everything for the cause.

**Are the Feminine Brigades of Saint Joan of Arc still active today?**

No. Once the truce was signed, the group was broken up so the the members could return to their respective homes and lead normal lives.

**Did the Mexican Knights of Columbus support the Cristiada?**

The first Knights of Columbus council in Mexico was established in 1905. Even in the anticlerical atmosphere of revolutionary-era Mexico, the Order grew to more than fifty councils in only six years. They set up schools and hospitals and funded religious education. As in the United States, the Knights (or "Caballeros" as they are known in Mexico) attracted bishops, priests, doctors, lawyers and other community leaders who were both staunchly Catholic and politically active.

Although the Knights as an organization could not officially support the Cristiada, over half of the founding members of the National League for the Defense of Religious Liberty were Knights of Columbus and hundreds became officers of its centers.

Accordingly, the Knights were specifically targeted by the government. Their magazine, *Columbia*, was banned, they were denied employment in state offices, many were expelled from their homes, and others were summarily executed—all for merely belonging to the Order.

In his 1926 encyclical letter *Iniquis Afflictisque*, Pope Pius XI singled out the Knights of Columbus as an organization "made up of active and industrious members, who because of their zeal in assisting the Church, have brought great honor upon themselves."

About seventy Knights are known to have been among the Cristeros killed during the war. To date, six Knights of Columbus have been canonized saints, and three more beatified, as martyrs of the Cristiada.

**Where did most of the confrontations between Cristeros and Federales take place?**

After the first successful defense in Los Altos, Jalisco, other states also began to coordinate their own organized defense. What started in Jalisco spread to surrounding states such as Zacatecas, Michoacan, Durango, Colima, Guanajuato, and Querétaro, spreading through most of the country soon after.

**Isn't waging war against Catholic teaching?**

Not if it falls under the Church's definition of a "just war." This doctrine was first enunciated by Saint Augustine of Hippo (A.D. 354—430). Over the centuries it was refined by Doctors of the Church, especially Saint Thomas Aquinas, and formally embraced by the Magisterium. The Church has also adapted the "just war theory" to the situation of modern warfare.

Certain conditions established by the Church must be met for a conflict to be considered a "just war." The Catholic Church's understanding of the "just war theory," is contained in paragraphs 2302—2317 of the *Catechism of the Catholic Church.*

**Did the Catholic Church support the Cristero movement?**

The Catholic bishops of Mexico could not get involved directly with the movement due to the Church's moral position on what constitutes a "just war." They did, however, support nonviolent measures, such as boycotts and petition drives, which did not involve taking up arms.

**What where the bishops of Mexico doing to help the Catholic community?**

The bishops worked diligently to have the Calles Law amended. Pope Pius XI explicitly approved this course of action. In September the episcopate submitted a proposal for the amendment of the Constitution of 1917, but Congress rejected it.

Failing to come to an agreement with the Calles regime, and in order to avoid any possible confrontations or bloodshed, the bishops of Mexico asked the Holy See for permission to suspend all Catholic celebration/worship on July 31, 1926, the eve before this new law would go into effect. *For Greater Glory* depicts the many marriages, baptisms, etc., that were celebrated en masse before the cessation of Church ceremonies.

The bishops continued to work tirelessly for a peaceful resolution as the war intensified, but each time they were turned away and their requests denied. During the fiercest persecutions, the clergy were hunted and tormented more than anyone. All the bishops risked arrest or execution for publicly criticizing the Calles law and the government. Most of them had to flee to the United States, where they received support from the U.S. bishops. Only two or three remained in Mexico.

**Who was Pope at the time of the persecution?**

Pope Pius XI was the Vicar of Christ during this period.

## What did the Holy See do to help the Church in Mexico?

When the oppression was about to begin, the Vatican granted permission, requested by the Mexican bishops, to cease any Catholic religious services in order to avoid confrontations. Additionally, the Holy See wrote letters to the government requesting they abolish the Calles Law. The government would ignore each request.

As the war intensified, Rome continued to have direct communications with President Calles to ask for leniency. Not only were Vatican officials dismissed, but diplomatic relations were broken off by the government.

Lastly, Pope Pius XI wrote an encyclical letter to the clergy and the faithful of Mexico to give them courage and hope during this persecution. There was really not much else the Holy See could do. On November 18, 1926, the Pope sent the encyclical letter *Iniquis Afflictisque* (*On the Persecution of the Church in Mexico*) to offer prayers and encouragement during this difficult time.

Cristeros from Southern Mexico

## THREE—U.S. INVOLVEMENT

**What did the United States know of the persecution of the Church in Mexico and what was its response?**

It is well to remember that while the Bill of Rights and the U.S. Constitution enshrine the right to religious liberty, anti-Catholic sentiment was strong in 1920s America. Margaret Sanger, foundress of Planned Parenthood, vigorously supported Calles' persecution of the Church, as did the Ku Klux Klan (KKK). In the KKK's widely distributed *The Knights of the Klan vs. the Knights of Columbus,* the radical racist group ridiculed Catholic immigrants as "ignorant and superstitious." They even went so far as to offer their four million members as soldiers for the Calles regime should any other group or nation try to intervene militarily on behalf of the Church.

The American government was certainly well aware of the persecution, but it did little initially, due to the vital U.S. interest in reestablishing crucial oil imports which President Calles had halted soon after taking power. At the same time, American Catholics staunchly supported their Catholic brethren in Mexico.

**Was the Catholic Church in the United States extending any assistance to Catholic Clergy during this persecution?**

The U.S. Catholic bishops extended their full support to

51

any clergy seeking assistance. It was a blessing in time of need for hundreds, if not thousands, of clergy and religious. Many clergy seeking asylum were welcomed by the U.S. Bishops and received accommodations, health services, food, and lodging during this time. Only two or three bishops stayed in Mexico in hiding; while others had to flee or were evicted to their own country of origin.

It is known that thousands of Catholics fled to other places such as the United States, Cuba, and Spain, among others, to escape this persecution. Not only regular lay people but also the many religious were exiled as their convents and seminaries were confiscated by the state.

**In the film, President Calvin Coolidge (played by Bruce McGill) speaks of "pressure from the Knights of Columbus" as an incentive for U.S. diplomats to convince Calles to end his "war against the Catholic Church." What did the U.S. Knights of Columbus do to stand with Catholics in Mexico?**

In August 1926, just days after the Calles Law took effect, the U.S. Knights passed a resolution to support the Church in Mexico. They established a fund that raised over a million dollars to offer relief services for those exiled from Mexico, to provide for exiled seminarians to continue their priestly formation, and to educate the American public about the true situation.

The Order printed and distributed five million pamphlets about the Cristiada and two million copies of the *Pastoral Letter of the Catholic Episcopate of the United States on the Religious Situation in Mexico*. The U.S. Knights also sponsored over 700 free lectures and reached millions by radio.

**Who was Dwight D. Morrow?**

Morrow (played by Bruce Greenwood in *For Greater Glory*) was appointed United States Ambassador to Mexico from 1927 to 1930 by then-President Calvin Coolidge. He was widely hailed as a brilliant diplomat, mixing popular appeal with sound financial advice.

**What was the result of Morrow's embassy?**

Ambassador Morrow was instrumental in bringing about the end of the persecution. He initiated a series of breakfast meetings with President Calles at which the two would discuss a range of issues, from the religious uprising to oil and irrigation. This earned him the nickname "the ham and eggs diplomat" in U.S. papers.

Morrow wanted the conflict to end both for regional security as a solution to the oil problem in the United States. In one meeting with Calles, the ambassador offered military support in exchange for oil so that Mexico could finish the war once and for all. In the end, however, he depended upon the diplomatic skill of Catholic clergy and laymen to negotiate the peace agreement which ended the Cristiada. He was aided in his efforts by Father John J.

Burke of the National Catholic Welfare Conference. The Holy See was also actively suing for peace.

After the assassination of Calles' successor, President Álvaro Obregon, the Mexican Congress appointed Portes Gil as interim president in September 1928. Gil was more open to the Church than Calles had been, allowing Morrow and Father Burke to reinstitute their peace initiative.

Portes Gil told a foreign correspondent on May 1, 1929, "The Catholic clergy, when they wish, may renew the exercise of their rites with only one obligation, that they respect the laws of the land."

Calles arm-in-arm with Calvin Coolidge (right)

# FOUR—CHARACTERS OF THE CRISTIADA

## Who was Anacleto González Flores and what role did he play during the persecution?

Blessed Anacleto González Flores (portrayed in the film by Eduardo Verástegui) was born on July 13, 1888, in Tepatitlán, Jalisco, Mexico. He grew up to be one of the leaders who coordinated and strategized the boycotts during the Cristiada. Blessed Anacleto was inspired by Mahatma Ghandi's example of "passive resistance" and is sometimes known as the "Mexican Ghandi." He was beatified by Benedict XVI as a martyr on November 20, 2005.

Blessed Anacleto was greatly involved in social and religious activities and was an enthusiastic member of the Catholic Association of Young Mexicans, or Asociación Católica de Juventud Mexicana (ACJM). He taught catechism, was dedicated to works of charity, and wrote many articles and books with a Christian spirit. In 1922 he married María Concepción Guerrero and they had two children.

By 1926, the situation in Mexico had worsened. Up until this time, Anacleto had advocated passive, nonviolent resistance, but he joined the cause of the National League for the Defense of Religious Liberty upon learning of the murder of four members of the ACJM.

In January 1927, guerrilla warfare spread throughout Jalisco. From his many hiding places Anacleto wrote and sent bulletins and coordinated efforts for peaceful resistance. He was eventually captured on an April morning in 1927 at the home of the Vargas González family, along with the three Vargas brothers. *For Greater Glory* employs some artistic license portraying Anacleto's martyrdom. He was not summarily executed as depicted in the film. After his arrest, he was taken to Fort Colorado where his torture included being hung by his thumbs until his fingers were dislocated and having the bottom of his feet slashed. He refused, however, to supply his captors with any information. José Anacleto González Flores was then shot, together with the Vargas González brothers and Luis Padilla Gómez, that same day, April 1, 1927.

It is worthy to note that in May 1925, Anacleto González Flores and Miguel Gómez Loza received the Pro Ecclesia Et Pontifice Award for their noble and generous works of service to the Catholic Church.

## Who was Miguel Gómez Loza?

Miguel Gómez Loza (played by Raul Mendez in *For Greater Glory*) was born on August 11, 1888, in Tepatitlán, Jalisco, Mexico. From a young age he displayed a strong love for God and a sincere devotion to the Blessed Virgin Mary. At age twenty-six Miguel entered the University of Morelos where he earned a law degree, eventually opening an office in Arandas, Jalisco, as an attorney.

In 1915 he became a member of the ACJM, and in 1919 he established a national congress of Catholic workers to unify industrial workers, commercial employees, and agricultural laborers. He also worked tirelessly to defend the rights of the needy. In consequence he was arrested fifty-nine times for organizing protests against the government.

In 1922 Miguel married María Guadalupe Sánchez Barragán and they had three children. He joined the National League for the Defense of Religious Liberty in 1927, but he continued to believe in a nonviolent approach to resist the persecution.

After the death of Anacleto, he was appointed, by Catholics, as Governor of Jalisco and strove by all the means at his disposal to defend liberty and justice. By March of 1928, Miguel was living on a ranch near Atotonilco, Jalisco. On March 21, 1928, federal forces, who were hunting for him, discovered his whereabouts. He was executed by firing squad the same day.

**Who led the Cristeros?**

At the beginning, leaders of the National League for the Defense of Religious Liberty took charge of the Cristero movement but lacked vision and experience. After a few major blows to their stronghold locations, they hired a mercenary general to take command of the Cristero forces.

## Who was General Enrique Gorostieta?

Enrique Gorostieta Velarde (portrayed in the film by Andy Garcia) was born in the state of Monterrey, Mexico, in 1889.  He received his military education at the Chapultepec Military College (known as the "Mexican West Point") and fought during the Revolution, becoming a successful combat general.  He was a decorated officer with an impressive history of triumphs.

Now retired from active duty, he used his knowledge of chemistry to secure employment as an engineer with a soap company.  The National League for the Defense of Religious Liberty sought out his leadership.

Ironically, Enrique Gorostieta was both an anticleric and a high-ranking Mason.  His initial motives for joining the Cristero movement, were the defense of religious freedom,  the high salary offered by the National League, and the furtherance of  his own political ambitions.

The Cristeros suffered from a lack of experience and military discipline which created difficult and oftentimes costly confrontations.   Gorostieta's firm direction as a Cristero general would bring much-needed organization to the insurgency.   He is credited with turning the Cristeros from a collection of motley outlaw bands into a disciplined Cristero army.   Under his direction the Cristeros were never defeated in the field.

They won a series of battles in rural Jalisco, Michoacan, Colima, and Zacatecas.  However, without support from the bishops of Mexico or the Vatican, and torn by internal dissension, the Cristeros never reached their full potential as a political or military force.

Gorostieta reacted sharply when word reached him about the U.S. Ambassador's attempt to negotiate a diplomatic settlement between the government and the Catholic Church. He immediately sent a strong letter to the bishops about this potential truce. He wrote:

*"Since the beginning of our uprising we continue to hear from the press about a possible truce between the Church and the government to end this religious conflict.*

*"Every time such articles get published, the men in battle have felt a deathly chill invade our souls. And each time we read of a bishop who is willing to negotiate with Calles, we receive such news like a slap on our face, and yet more painful as it comes from those from whom we hope to receive some type of moral support, a word of encouragement, which up to now, we have received none."*

The government, seeing Gorostieta as a stumbling block to the potential truce, put a higher reward on his head. On June 2, 1929, Gorostieta was killed following a government intelligence operation, just three weeks before the truce was signed.

With the movement rapidly collapsing, Gorostieta had attempted a retreat into Michoacan, where he hoped to recruit followers and continue the rebellion. A federal officer, who had infiltrated Gorostieta's inner circle, tipped off the Mexican cavalry to the general's presence in

Atotonilco, Jalisco. He was killed there in a short firefight. The anniversary of his death is still celebrated in Mexico today by a large group of his followers.

## Was Gorsotieta's wife really named Tula or Tulita?

Yes. The full name of General Gorostieta's wife was Gertrudis Lazaga Sepulveda (played by Eva Longoria in *For Greater Glory*). Tula would be the appropriate nickname for someone named Gertrudis. She might also be called Tulita as a term of endearment.

## Who was José Sánchez del Río?

José Sánchez del Río was a young Cristero soldier (played in *For Greater Glory* by Mauricio Kuri). José was horrified to witness personally the persecution of local priests and the desecration of churches in his small hometown of Sahuayo, Michoacan.

When the Cristero War broke out in 1926, his older brothers took up arms and joined the movement, but his mother would not allow José to take part. The Cristero general, Prudencio Mendoza, also refused his enlistment. But, in the end, Mendoza finally relented and allowed José to become the flag bearer of the troop.

José was known to be one of the youngest members of the Cristero movement. He was nicknamed "Tarcisius" by the Cristeros after the early Christian boy martyr who gave his life to protect the Eucharist from desecration.

During heavy fighting on January 25, 1928, General Mendoza's horse was shot out from under him. In an act of great heroism and sacrifice, José gave his own horse to the general so that the battle could go on. He then sought cover and fired at the enemy until he ran out of ammunition. Government troops captured the boy and imprisoned him in the sacristy of the local church.

Forced to watch the execution of a fellow Cristero, José could not be made to break his resolve not to reveal any intelligence. The following is from an alleged eyewitness account of José's gruesome martyrdom on February 10, 1928:

*"Consequently they cut the bottom of his feet and obliged him to walk around the town toward the cemetery. They also at times cut him with a machete until he was bleeding from several wounds. He cried and moaned with pain, but he did not give in. At times they stopped him and said, 'If you shout 'Death to Christ the King' we will spare your life.' José would only shout, 'I will never give in. ¡Viva Cristo Rey!' When they reached the place of execution, they stabbed him numerous times with bayonets. He only shouted louder, '¡Viva Cristo Rey!'"*

The government commander was so furious that he pulled out his pistol and shot José in the head. He was declared a martyr and was beatified by Pope Benedict XVI on November 20, 2005.

## Did José Sánchez del Río and General Gorostieta really have the close relationship portrayed in the movie?

The dramatic arc of the film depicts an ever-closer friendship between Enrique Gorostieta and the young Cristero José Sánchez del Río. Their relationship is a plot device to portray Gorostieta's journey from "the last man to believe in their cause" to a committed Cristero willing to die for it.

Historically, Gorostieta and José did not know each other personally. Despite this artistic license however, the basic outline of their actions and sacrifices is accurate. For example, the film depicts young José Sánchez del Río surrendering his horse to Victoriano Ramirez ("El Catorce") during a fierce battle. In actual fact he gave his horse to General Prudencio Mendoza, a commander of the troops to which he belonged.

## Who was Victoriano Ramirez also known as "El Catorce"?

General Victoriano Ramirez also known as "El Catorce" (Spanish for "The fourteen"), was a "ranchero" who became a famous fighter during the Cristiada. He was one of the first men to join the armed resistance and led various attacks in the region of San Julian in the state of Jalisco. But he was also a "rebel among rebels."

## Did Ramirez really kill fourteen soldiers as in the film?

According to the testimony of historians of the Cristiada, a local police chief sent fourteen Federales to capture Ramirez, dead or alive. As depicted in the film, he successfully avoided capture by killing all fourteen of his assailants. He then strung their guns together on a rope and sent them to the police chief with the message, "If you want to capture me, next time you'd better send more than fourteen." It was this incident that earned him the sobriquet "El Catorce."

**Did Ramirez fight alongside General Gorostieta? And were there tensions between them?**

Ramirez did indeed fight alongside Gorostieta but would oftentimes disobey orders or defiantly question the more experienced general's military strategies. Ramirez wanted to have complete command of his own men and did not countenance any interference. So when the Cristeros hired General Gorostieta, he became jealous and insubordinate. That, in addition to other decisions and actions that ran contrary to the Cristeros' larger plans, did not bode well regarding his future in the movement.

Unlike the heroic death pictured in the film, it is reported that "El Catorce" was executed on March 17, 1929, by men from his own unit to avoid further setbacks.

**Father José Reyes Vega (portrayed by Santiago Cabrera in *For Greater Glory*) was a Cristero General. Can a priest legitimately wage war?**

The short answer is no. Priests depend on the power of prayer and the grace of Almighty God - they don't depend on bullets. As Saint Thomas Aquinas writes in the *Summa Theologica*:

*"[It] is the duty of clerics to dispose and counsel other men to engage in just wars. For they are forbidden to take up arms, not as though it were a sin, but because such an occupation is unbecoming their personality. [...] Although it is meritorious to wage a just war, nevertheless it is rendered unlawful for clerics, by reason of their being deputed to works more meritorious still. [For example] the marriage act may be meritorious; and yet it becomes reprehensible in those who have vowed virginity, because they are bound to a yet greater good."*

This, however, does not keep priests from acting as chaplains to the military. As the Angelic Doctor also states:

*"Prelates and clerics may, by the authority of their superiors, take part in wars, not indeed by taking up arms themselves, but by affording spiritual help to those who fight justly, by exhorting and absolving them, and by other like spiritual helps."*

It would seem this could also apply to clergy such as Bishop José Francisco Orozco of Guadalajara. Unwilling to leave his flock, the bishop remained with the rebels while formally rejecting armed rebellion.

**Father Vega mentions in the beginning of the film, *"But the Bible also says there is a time for peace and a time for war."* Where in the Bible is this verse?**

Ecclesiastes 3:8

**Did Father Vega remain a priest?**

Yes. Like Baptism and Confirmation, the sacrament of Holy Orders confers an indelible character on the soul; hence, the old saying, "Once a priest, always a priest." We are also informed at the end of *For Greater Glory* that Father Vega had the benefit of sacramental confession before he died.

**The character of Father Vega hears the confession of General Gorostieta near the end of the film. Given Father Vega's irregular condition as a "fighting priest" would that confession have been valid?**

Although the Church had officially suspended religious services, and Father Vega was illegitimately participating in combat, his celebration of the Holy Sacrifice of the Mass would have remained valid, but not licit.

The sacrament of Penance, on the other hand, requires faculties (a special permission) from the local ordinary for validity. However, in a situation where there is danger of death, the Church itself supplies faculties so that even an excommunicated priest can validly hear someone's confession in an emergency. Presumably, the situation portrayed in the film would fall under this category.

**In the film there is a scene where people were burned alive in a train by order of Father Vega. Did that really occur?**

Accounts vary as to how many lives were actually lost and who was to blame for this incident. Of course, there are two sides to every story.

The Cristeros maintained that everyone was evacuated before the train was engulfed in flames. In the film, Father Vega is stunned to hear the screams of people still trapped inside the train. The Calles regime insisted that Cristeros purposely set the train on fire with everyone aboard, killing fifty-one people, including women and children.

A third version relates that government officials put people on the train, set it on fire, and then blamed the Cristeros in order to justify a continued and even fiercer persecution. Only God knows the truth. In the end, real or imagined, this episode was a real blow to public opinion about the Cristeros.

**Is it true that some other Cristeros committed atrocities against the human dignity of innocent persons?**

This is a common charge against militant Catholic action whatever the era. The topics of the Crusades, the Inquisitions, the Cristiada, etc., always invite the charge of hypocrisy against Catholics and the Church. The plain fact is that human beings are not perfect, and injustices happen even among those with the best intentions.

Extant personal testimonies reveal that some Cristeros took advantage of the conflict to commit various levels of crime, as soldiers have always done throughout history. It is truly a shame that any Cristero would abuse the situation to commit such crimes. However, it is crucial to remember that, whatever the evil actions of a few, thousands more courageous men and women willingly fought, sacrificed, and even gave their lives for Christ the King!

It is also important to mention that there was a large group of men who looked like Cristeros but in reality were peasants working for the government to create confusion and turn public opinion against the Cristeros. They committed atrocious crimes and told their victims explicitly, "You have just been robbed by Cristeros!"

**How many lives were lost during this persecution?**

The exact number cannot be accurately calculated. It is said that the Cristeros lost over 25,000 men while the government lost over 65,000 troops during the war. Altogether the deaths attributable to this conflict, and the persecution that provoked and encouraged it, may reach as high as 200,000.

**How many of those killed are considered martyrs for the**

**Catholic Faith?**

The Catholic Church has canonized twenty-five martyrs of the Cristiada and beatified fifteen more, but there are many others who may be on the path to sainthood in the years ahead. There are perhaps thousands of others whose stories of sacrifice for Holy Mother Church will never be known. Only God truly knows the sanctity of each one of them.

**Are there any recorded last words of the Cristero martyrs?**

Yes. Blessed José Sánchez del Río's last words before his execution were, "Tell my parents I will see them in heaven. ¡Viva Cristo Rey!"

Blessed Anacleto González Flores' last words came as he was hung by his thumbs, flogged, and stabbed by a bayonet. He forgave his executioners and gave them the order to fire their weapons at the cry of "¡Viva Cristo Rey!"

As seven soldiers lined up to fire upon his beaten body he said, "Listen, Americas for the second time: I die, but God does not die. ¡Viva Cristo Rey!"

**What was the origin of Blessed Anacleto's final words?**

One of Blessed Anacleto's heroes was the martyred Ecuadoran president, Gabriel García Moreno. After being elected for a third term as president of Ecuador, García

Moreno was warned that his life would be in jeopardy. He knew the risk and he took it.

On August 5, 1875, in the Plaza Grande of Quito, Ecuador, García Moreno was mortally wounded by a group of anti-Catholic assassins. When told by one of his murderers, "We have won. We have killed God," García Moreno cried out, "Listen, Americas: I die, but God does not die. ¡Viva Cristo Rey!"

When Blessed Anacleto was about to be executed he repeated the words of his hero, calling upon the Americas to witness for a second time God's eternal Presence in the face of atheistic tyranny.

Blesseds José Sánchez del Río and Anacleto Gonzáles Flores

Enrique Gorostieta and a "Capitana Brigadista"

Father Vega

## FIVE – FREEDOM IS OUR LIVES

**How did the persecution end?**

The end of this persecution finally came about under the pressure of U.S. Ambassador Dwight Morrow who wanted to serve as a peacemaker, but also to gain political favors. The Mexican bishops and the Holy See were also willing to negotiate to stop the bloodshed and the persecution of the innocent.

**Who won the Cristiada? Was there "victory" for the Cristeros?**

It is very difficult to identify a "winner" in this religious battle. In the end, Catholics regained the freedom to practice their faith and some (though not all) Church property. But at what cost? Thousands of widows and orphans suffered greatly for many years after the war ended. If indeed there is a winner of this tragic episode, it would have to be all the Mexican citizens born after the conflict who enjoy the freedom to practice their Faith.

The religious liberty that exists in Mexico today—and everywhere throughout the world where religious persecution has occurred—is mostly due to those who gave their lives fighting to keep it. As the early Church Father Tertullian (d. A.D. 255) proclaimed: *"The blood of the martyrs is the seed of the Church."*

## Was there a definitive "end date" of the Cristero War?

Yes, there was a definitive end date. June 23, 1929, is the official date of the signing of the truce between the bishops and the government negotiated by Ambassador Morrow and Father Burke. At this time the bishops ordered the National League for the Defense of Religious Liberty to cease military and political activities and the Cristeros to lay down their weapons.

## Were the Cristeros safe after the truce?

Sadly, the truce which was signed between the Mexican government and the Catholic Church was indeed also a trap for the Cristeros. Many knew it was a trap but were tired of fighting. Although not all obliged, the majority left their destiny in God's hands and followed orders to abandon the battlefield and surrender their weapons.

The regime quickly broke the promise to abide by the agreed-to terms. During the first three months after the truce was signed, Calles had over five hundred Cristero leaders and 5,000 common Cristeros shot. More Cristero leaders died in this brief period of time than during the entire three-year war. The murders continued from June 1929 through September of the same year.

## Did President Calles' successors continue persecuting the Church? Were they just as militant in their anti-Catholicism?

Calles' presidency ended in 1928 while the persecution was at its fiercest level. His successor, Emilio Portes Gil, realized the grave error Calles had made by enforcing the anticlerical laws. However, Calles—the "Jefe Supremo"—was really still in control and would not agree to change the policy until it became evident that the war had to end. The end of the war did not mean an end to persecution, however.

There was a second popular uprising in the early 1930s in response to the renewed persecution. In 1932, Pope Pius XI wrote a second encyclical letter titled *Acerba Animi* ("*Sorrow of the Soul*") with the same purpose as his previous encyclical—to give courage and blessings to the faithful. This latter persecution was thankfully neither as fierce nor as prolonged as the Cristiada.

**Are there any survivors of the Cristiada alive today?**

Yes, but very few. Those who survived this persecution and are old enough to remember are probably in their 90s today. However, in the little rural towns and villages, one can still see simple shrines devoted to the local priest who stood up for his flock and had been martyred as a result. There is a stark contrast between the deep and unwavering devotion among some people and the almost complete lack of awareness among the majority. It is to be hoped that *For Greater Glory: The True Story of Cristiada* will help bridge that gap.

**Is there any mention of the Cristiada in Mexico's public school text books today?**

Not as much as one would expect. As recently as the 1980s it was difficult to find a single book that mentioned anything substantive about the Cristiada. If it was mentioned, it usually was no more than a single sentence in President Calles' biography. If the school system did not include the Cristiada as part of its history, future generations would soon lose any knowledge of it. Naturally, this was before the Internet was developed.

But even today it is important to note a crucial difference between the official state narrative and the Catholic understanding of events. The Mexican government portrays the Cristiada as a rebellion because the Cristeros "rebelled" against the enforcement of the Calles Law. But rebellion is hardly a fitting way to describe an attempt to restore customs in place for centuries before the Mexican Revolution.

Catholics see the Cristiada as a response, albeit a violent one, to unjust persecution because Catholics were persecuted by unjust laws that inhibited their religious freedom. Today, Mexican school textbooks include this chapter in the country's history, however, they do not refer to it as a "persecution" of Catholics but rather a "rebellion" by Catholics. Yet, there is also more freedom of the press today, and a large volume of untold stories about the Cristiada—testimonies and images that were illegal to print or publish for many years—are finally emerging. There are literally thousands of testimonies coming to light that reveal an inspiring history that has been hidden for decades under a dark shadow of fear and denial.

**Are there any limitations to freedom of religion and worship in Mexico today?**

Diplomatic relations between Mexico and the Holy See were reestablished in 1992. Still, the anticlerical laws remain in Mexico's Constitution, but—according to a mutual agreement—will not be applied to its citizens. As to "limitations," many priests in Mexico still do not wear clerical garb in public due to the tradition begun when such garb was outlawed during the persecution.

**Is persecution, albeit on a less overt level, still taking place in Mexico?**

Yes. Priests and Catholic Churches are still under attack in Mexico by the secular media. Also, according to a survey conducted throughout the entire Church in Mexico: during current President Felipe Calderon's leadership, twelve priests and two seminarians have been assassinated, 162 priests have received death threats, and nearly a thousand priests have been the victims of extortion.

**Is there any parallel between what happened in Mexico during the Cristero persecution and what is happening**

**right now in the United States (e.g., Catholics ordered to violate their conscience and moral teachings to comply with federal insurance coverage mandates)?**

Yes, there is certainly a parallel. Some forces in American politics already treat freedom of religion as "freedom from religion." The question is, "What are Catholics in the United States today willing to do to defend their religious liberty?" The answer may surprise us all.

**What good can be said to have come out of the Cristiada?**

This has always been hard to explain because of the pain and devastation it left behind, especially for those who lost loved ones. But God will always bring good out of any evil situation. That is our hope in Christ and His Holy Will.

First, had it not been for these courageous men and women who stood up to defend their religious freedom, Mexico would be a Socialist/Communist country today. This is by all accounts a certainty. God only knows what this would mean to its citizens and its neighboring countries.

Secondly, Mexico has given the world, especially the United States, a priceless Catholic heritage through its culture, devotion to Our Lady of Guadalupe, and generations of many great priests.

Lastly, when thousands of religious were evicted from Mexico as the Calles Law was enforced, many of them founded houses of prayer, convents, religious orders, and seminaries, bringing and spreading many graces and blessings to the neighboring countries. Established by Venerable Mother Luisita Josefa of the Most Blessed Sacrament, the Carmelite Sisters of the Most Blessed Sacrament of Los Angeles was one of those orders. According to their official website:

*"In the 1920's during the revolution and religious persecution in Mexico in the beginning days of our Congregation, our Foundress, Mother Maria Luisa Josefa of the Most Blessed Sacrament became a light in that darkness of confusion and hatred. She established schools, hospitals, and orphanages. The very persecution which sought to destroy her work only spread it to another land, our own United States. Her ideal of combining contemplation with apostolic love taught her daughters to cling to God in mind and heart, while associating themselves with the work of Redemption and spreading the Kingdom of God.*

*"On July 1, 2000, our Holy Father, Pope John Paul II, promulgated that Mother Maria Luisa Josefa be called "Venerable," which means that it has been proven that Mother Luisita practiced her virtues to an heroic degree. She is now a candidate for beatification which requires evidence of one miracle through her intercession."*

So the answer to the question, "Did any good come from the Cristiada?" should be a resounding yes!

**What can be done to ensure that a situation like the Cristiada does not happen again – in Mexico or here in America?**

The answer lies in studying history and contemplating the consequences that ensue when good men do nothing. Catholics clearly need to be vigilant and stand firm for the Faith and be ready to contend for our religious freedom at all costs.

The epistle of Saint Jude exhorts us to "Contend earnestly for the faith once delivered to the saints" (Jude 1:3). Catholics know this means storming heaven with prayers, for we can achieve nothing apart from God (cf. John 1:5). But it also means to take action – perhaps even to give our lives for future generations if it is required - because "faith without works is dead" (James 2:26).

A world where more and more historically Christian nations seek to redefine religious freedom to mean only "freedom of worship" inside our own "temples" is only a step away from a world in which actually living the faith will be a crime.

Blessed John Paul II taught that "Those who posses certain rights have a duty to defend them." Catholics around the world today who strive to live in a way that reflects their faith in every aspect of life should echo the words of General Enrique Gorostieta in *For Greater Glory*, "Freedom is our lives. ¡Viva Cristo Rey!"

# FOR GREATER GLORY
## PHOTO GALLERY

———————

Mauricio Kuri as José Sánchez del Río.

José (Mauricio Kuri) in the Cristero camp with General Gorostieta, portrayed by Academy Award® Nominee, Andy Garcia

José (Mauricio Kuri) on the way to his execution. Below: José (Kuri) held by his mother (Karyme Lozano, right) after his martyrdom.

Academy Award® Nominee, Andy Garcia as General
Enrique Gorostieta Velarde.

Gorostieta (Gracia) with his wife Tulita played by Golden Globe Winner Eva Longoria. Below: Gorostieta with Victoriano "El Catorce" Ramirez (right) played by Oscar Isaac.

Golden Globe Winner Eva Longoria as Tulita. Below:
Tulita (Longoria, center) with her daughters.

Father Vega portrayed by Santiago Cabrera. Below: Father Vega (Cabrera, center) says Holy Mass for the Cristeros.

Eduardo Verástegui portrays Blessed Anacleto Gonzalez Flores.

Catalina Sandino Moreno as Adriana. Below: Adriana (Moreno, center) with Blessed Anacleto (Eduardo Verástegui, left with beard).

Oscar Isaac portrays Victoriano "El Catorce" Ramirez.
Below: Nestor Carbonell as Mayor Picazo.

Rubén Blades as President Plutarco Elías Calles.

# BONUS ESSAY
## AND
# CRISTERO PRAYERS

———————

# Who Can Be a Priest? — The Question That Killed 200,000 Mexicans

Carl Anderson, Supreme Knight, Knights of Columbus

From haunting photographs of hangings, to the movie *For Greater Glory,* once you've seen the horrors of the Mexican persecution and the Cristero rebellion, it is hard to forget them. But let us also not forget how seemingly mild the state's first injustices against the Church really were.

Religious persecution rarely begins with blood. It begins with redefinition—redefinition of the religion's role in personal lives, in ministers, in churches, in society and in government. In Mexico's case, the clergy were the state's first target. It began with a simple statement: all priests must register with the state. The problem was that, by this law, the state gave itself the authority to determine who was a minister and who was not.

A state that can decide ministers can also decide what doctrines it will permit to be preached. Priests and religious were forbidden from criticizing the government. Catholic schools were closed. Priests were refused even the basic rights of other citizens, including the right to vote and the right to testify in a trial – if convicted of disobeying the religious laws.

A State that does not believe in vowed celibacy for priests, nuns, or brothers must necessarily exclude them as ministers, too. And thus all monasteries were closed in Mexico, forcing hundreds to seek other homes.

With the authority to determine who is a minister, the state also afforded itself the power to determine how many ministers were allowed in each area. Hundreds of thousands were left without priests.

Step by step, the government advanced a plan of controlling Catholicism, by "purifying" the religion of involvement by "foreigners," and by controlling its message.

The state essentially attempted to create a "Catholic Church" which was not "catholic," in the international sense. Expelling foreign-born priests—whom we commonly call missionaries—the state rejected the missionary dimension of the faith—the call to "preach to all nations."

Similarly, although the Mexican government publically later denied it wanted to suppress Our Lady of Guadalupe, it is doubtful whether Calles' regime would be as supportive of who she really is: the Mother of the Americas, from Canada to Argentina.

What began as a "minor" issue—the government manipulation of who could register as clergy—very soon struck at the heart of Catholic identity, by attempting to introduce in its place something that, unlike the Catholic

Church, was not "one, holy, catholic and apostolic." Rather, it was disunified, unholy, national rather than universal, and distinctly broken from apostolic succession.

In seeking to eliminate the political voice of the clergy, the state politicized religion. In an attempt to enforce strict division of Church and state, the state made religion a weapon of the state with the mission—not of preaching Christ but—of strong-arming Mexicans into a form of Christianity that was purely devotional and purely Mexican.

As President Calles told Bishop Pasqual Díaz of Tabasco, who appealed to freedom of conscience in a meeting regarding the issue, "The law is above the dictates of conscience."

Calles wasn't alone in governing this way. Across the Ocean in Europe, these pretensions were well summarized by Benito Mussolini in 1919 when he said, "Everything within the state, nothing outside the state, nothing against the state."

At every step of the way, the state ran into problems with the "minor" legal hurdles it forced on the Church when, in order to enforce the law, it had to use force.

What is most sad is that the state had tried this path before. Realizing that the type of Catholic Church it would tolerate could not be Catholic, a year before Catholics took up arms in the Cristiada rebellion, the state established the nationalist "Mexican Catholic Apostolic Church"—

complete with a schismatic priest, "Patriarch Pérez." This reflected an earlier state-run "church" Calles established as governor before his presidency.

President Calles was essentially trying to nationalize religion, just as he was trying to nationalize Mexico's oil wealth. The international press even reported that there were plans to take over the Basilica of Our Lady of Guadalupe and make it a "Mexican Vatican" for the nationalist "Mexican Church."

In what can be seen as a trial run for the state's later repossession of churches during the Cristiada, the state closed La Soledad Church and turned it over to the new nationalist "Mexican Church." The plan didn't pan out—a riot ensued, forcing the government to withdraw "Patriarch Pérez."

The lesson of this failure wasn't lost on President Calles: what could not be replaced could perhaps be altered. Perhaps in Mexico he could force religion out of the public square and relegate religious practice to shrines and homes; he could create a cultural ghetto with strong legal walls. The Faith, however, doesn't reside in buildings, but in people. Thousands who stood up for the Faith, in various ways throughout the war, are testimony to that.

Among those singled out by Pope Pius XI for their service to the Church during this difficult time were the Knights of Columbus, who in Mexico provided a unique witness to the Catholic Church. As an international Catholic organization, the Knights were a reminder of the internationality of the Church, and of the unity of humanity.

The Knights of Columbus in Mexico—and in the United States—understood this attempt to suppress the public dimension of religion.

As persecution grew in Mexico leading up to the Calles Law, Knights in Mexico took upon themselves to further the charitable and missionary work of the Church: by funding hospitals and schools and supporting lay evangelization groups to spread the faith to those people unable to be reached by the clergy.

For the Knights of Columbus' Catholic activism and denouncement of the religious restrictions, the Mexican government added the Knights to its list of targets. Mexican government agents ransacked the Knights' headquarters in Mexico, banned its publication from the postal services, and killed over 70 Knights, including at least one simply for being a Knight. In addition to creating a nationalized "Mexican Church," the leaders in the state also created an alternative to the Knights of Columbus— the Knights of Guadalupe (which has no relation to the current group existing by that name). Unlike the Knights of Columbus who stood with the Catholic Church, one of the first missions of this parallel "Calles-sponsored" group was to help in the takeover of La Soledad Church for the Mexican government.

For the Knights of Columbus, the importance of the priestly ministry was never lost. In fact, the Order's close collaboration with priests is probably part of the reason for the Mexican government's targeting of the Knights of Columbus. (At least 20 of the 90 priests killed by the government during that period were Knights of Columbus, including many council chaplains.)

Many aspects of the Mexican Constitution and the Calles Law made living a public Catholic life difficult. Not only had priests been expelled and monasteries closed, but clerical garb had also been forbidden in public, as had public processions or other public religious displays.

Much of that was ancillary in the end. In June 1929, the agreement which ended the years of bloody war focused on just the question of ministerial definition.

The state promised to revise its interpretation of the law, promising not to register or list as priests anyone other than those the bishops wanted. It would also turn a blind eye to the Church's public expressions.

It was that simple. The present faith-filled lives of Mexicans today are due to the uncompromising faithfulness of those who lived and defended the Church during the persecution and the Cristiada. In the images of triumphs and tragedies, let us not only imagine the deaths. Let us remember who these people were. They were

Mexicans who believed in a Catholicism relevant to all peoples regardless of nationality, who believed in the sacredness of the priesthood, who believed in a missionary Church, who believed that the Virgin of Guadalupe is not only for Mexicans but is Queen of all the Americas.

They were a people who believed it is Christ through the Church Who calls men to the priesthood and changes their immortal souls with the words "You are a priest forever" and "Do this in memory of Me." To paraphrase St. Thomas More, they were Mexico's good subjects, but God's first. "Viva Cristo Rey!"

Carl Anderson is Supreme Knight of the Knights of Columbus and the co-author of *The New York Times* bestseller *Our Lady of Guadalupe: Mother of the Civilization of Love.*

# CRISTERO PRAYERS

**Prayer to Christ the King**

Christ Jesus, I acknowledge You as our Universal King. All that exists has been created by You. I renew my promises of my Baptism, renouncing Satan, his temptations, and his works, and I promise to be a good Christian. Most importantly, I promise, according to my means, to ensure the triumph of Your Will and Holy Mother Church .

Oh Jesus, I offer my humble actions so that every human heart acknowledges and lives Your message of peace, justice and love. Amen.

**Oración a Cristo Rey**

Oh Cristo Jesús, Te reconozco por Rey Universal. Todo cuanto existe ha sido creado por Ti. Renuevo mis promesas del bautismo, renunciando a Satanás, a sus seducciones, y a sus obras, y prometo vivir como buen cristiano. Muy en particular me comprometo a hacer triunfar, según mis medios, los derechos de Dios y de Tu Iglesia.

Jesucristo, Te ofrezco mis pobres acciones para obtener que

todos los corazones reconozcan y vivan Tu mensaje de paz, de justicia, y de amor. Amén.

## Battle Hymn of the Cristeros

(Sung to the tune of *Marcha Real*, the national anthem of Spain)

The Virgin Mary is our protector and defender when there is something to fear,
She will defeat the demons, crying, "Long live Christ the King!"
She will defeat the demons, crying, "Long live Christ the King!"
Soldiers of Christ, let us follow the flag that the Cross shows the army of God!
Let us follow the flag crying, "Long live Christ the King!"

## Combata Himno de la Cristeros

La Virgen María es nuestra protectora y nuestra defensora cuando hay que temer,
Vencerá a los demonios, gritando, "¡Viva Cristo Rey!",
Vencerá a los demonios, gritando, "¡Viva Cristo Rey!"
Soldados de Cristo: ¡Sigamos la bandera que la Cruz enseña el ejército de Dios!
Sigamos la bandera gritando, "¡Viva Cristo Rey!"

## Prayer to Blessed Anacleto González Flores

Merciful Jesus, my sins are only but the drops of Blood You shed for me. I am not worthy of being a part of the army that fights for the rights of Your Church. I wish to have never sinned so that my life would be a worthy offering before Your eyes. Wash me from my inequities and cleanse me from my sins. By Your Holy Cross and by Your Holy Blessed Mother of Guadalupe, forgive me. I have not made penance as I should for my sins, which is why I deserve to die, as due punishment for them. I don't want to fight, nor live, nor die unless it is for Your Holy Church. Holy Mother of Guadalupe, in my agony, do not abandon me. Grant that my last cry on earth and my first canticle in heaven be "Long Live Christ the King!" Amen.

## Oración a Anacleto González Flores

Jesús Misericordioso! Mis pecados son más que las gotas de Sangre que derramaste por mí. No merezco pertenecer al ejército que defiende los derechos de Tu Iglesia y que lucha por Ti. Quisiera nunca haber pecado para que mi vida fuera una ofrenda agradable a Tus ojos. Lávame de mis iniquidades y límpiame de mis pecados. Por Tu santa Cruz, por mi Madre Santísima de Guadalupe, perdóname, no he sabido hacer penitencia de mis pecados; por eso quiero recibir la muerte como un castigo merecido por ellos. No quiero pelear, ni vivir, ni morir, sino por Ti y por Tu Iglesia. Madre Santa de Guadalupe, acompaña en su agonía a este pobre pecador. Concéde que mi último grito en la tierra y mi primer cántico en el cielo sea "¡Viva Cristo Rey!" Amén.

## Prayer to Blessed José Sánchez del Río

Oh, Blessed José, the smallest soldier of Christ, whose last bloody steps led you to the arms of the Virgin Mary and our Lord, help our soldiers for Christ who are left here on earth maintain strong foothold in a way that they can persevere and resist until the end. Amen.

## Oración a José Sánchez del Río

Oh beato José, el más pequeño soldado de Cristo, cuyos últimos pasos sangrientos te llevaron a los brazos de la Virgen María y de nuestro Señor, manten sano y fuerte los pasos de los soldados de nuestro Señor, que permanecen aquí en la tierra de tal manera que pueda tener tu fuerza para resistir y perseverar hasta el fin. Amén.

## Novena Prayer to Blessed Miguel Agustin Pro, SJ

Blessed martyr of Christ the King, Father Miguel Agustin Pro, you are a special patron of those who labor, those in illness, depression, or despair. You are also a friend of musicians, the captives, and all who work toward social justice. Your beloved brothers, the Jesuits, revere you and count you among the ranks of their saints. You love your people of Mexico and all those loyal to the Church.

I thank the Sacred Heart for loving you so dearly. I pray to Our Lady of Guadalupe, whom you love so dearly, to intercede for the cause of your canonization. I pray that you remember me in your eternal and well-deserved rejoicing, and also my needs: [state needs]. Through your courageous life and martyrdom you have won the crown of life everlasting. Remember me, Blessed Miguel, for I remember you. Long live Christ the King! Long live Our Lady of Guadalupe!

**IMPRIMATUR: + Most Reverend John F. Donoghue Archbishop of Atlanta, December 21, 2004**

**Oración Para la Novena del Beato Miguel Agustin Pro, S.J.**

Beato mártir de Cristo Rey, Padre Miguel Agustin Pro, eres un patrón especial para aquellos quienes laboran, para los enfermos, o aquellos que se sufren de depresión o desesperación. Igual eres amigo de los músicos, los cautivos, y aquellos quienes luchan por los derechos sociales. Tus amadísimos hermanos, los Jesuitas, reverencian y te consideran entre los rangos de sus santos. Amaste tu gente de México y todos aquellos fieles a la iglesia.

Agradezco al Sagrado Corazón por haberte amado tanto. Le pido a la Virgen de Guadalupe a quién tanto amaste, que interceda por la causa de tu canonización. Pido que me recuerdes en tu eterno y bien merecido jubilo y por mis necesidades (Aquí se hacen sus peticiones). A través de tu valientoso ejemplo y martirio has ganado la corona de vida eternal. Recuérdame, Beato Miguel, que yo me acuerdo de ti. ¡Viva Cristo Rey! ¡Viva la Virgen de Guadalupe!

## SAINTS AND BLESSEDS OF THE CRISTIADA

St. Agustín Caloca

St. Atilano Cruz Alvarado

St. Cristobal Magallanes

St. David Galván Bermudes

St. David Roldán Lara

St. David Uribe Velasco

St. Jenaro Sánchez Delgadillo

St. Jesús Méndez Montoya

St. José Isabel Flores Varela

St. José Maria Robles Hurtado (Priest)*

St. Jóven Salvador Lara Puente

St. Julio Álvarez Mendoza

St. Justino Orona Madrigal

St. Luis Batiz Sáinz (Priest)*

St. Manuel Morales

St. Margarito Flores García

St. Mateo Correa Magallanes (Priest)*

St. Miguel De La Mora (Priest)*

St. Pedro de Jesús Maldonado Lucero (Priest)*

St. Pedro Esqueda Ramírez

St. Rodrigo Aguilar Alemán (Priest)*

St. Román Adame Rosales

St. Sabas Reyes Salazar

St. Tranquilino Ubiarco

St. Toribio Romo González

Blessed Anacleto González Flores

Blessed Andrés Solá Molist (Priest)*

Blessed Ángel Darío Acosta Zurita (Priest)

Blessed Ezequiel Huerta Gutiérrez

Blessed Jorge Vargas González

Blessed José Sánchez del Río

Blessed José Trinidad Rangel Montaño (Priest) *

Blessed Leonardo Pérez Larios *

Blessed Luis Magaña Servín

Blessed Luis Padilla Gómez

Blessed Miguel Gómez Loza

Blessed Mateo Elías del Socorro Nieves (Priest)

Blessed Miguel Agustin Pro Juárez (Priest)

Blessed Ramón Vargas González

Blessed Salvador Huerta Gutiérrez


* Indicates member of Knights of Columbus

# PAPAL ENCYCLICALS

# INIQUIS AFFLICTISQUE

## ENCYCLICAL OF POPE PIUS XI ON THE PERSECUTION OF THE CHURCH IN MEXICO TO THE VENERABLE BRETHREN, THE PATRIARCHS, PRIMATES, ARCHBISHOPS, BISHOPS, AND OTHER ORDINARIES IN PEACE AND COMMUNION WITH THE APOSTOLIC SEE.

**1.** In speaking to the Sacred College of Cardinals at the Consistory of last December, We pointed out that there existed no hope or possibility of relief from the sad and unjust conditions under which the Catholic religion exists today in Mexico except it be by a "special act of Divine Mercy." You, Venerable Brothers, did not delay to make your own and approve Our convictions and Our wishes in this regard, made known to you on so many occasions, for by every means within your power you urged all the faithful committed to your pastoral care to implore by instant prayers the Divine Founder of the Church that He bring some relief from the heavy burden of these great evils.

**2.** We designedly use the words "the heavy burden of these great evils" for certain of Our children, deserters from the army of Jesus Christ and enemies of the Common Father of all, have ordered and are continuing up to the present hour a cruel persecution against their own brethren, Our most beloved children of Mexico. If in the first centuries of our era and at other periods in history Christians were treated in a more barbarous fashion than now, certainly in no place or at no time has it happened before that a small group of men has so outraged the rights of God and of the Church as they are now doing in Mexico, and this without the slightest regard for the past glories of their country, with no feelings of pity for their fellow-citizens. They have also done away with the liberties of the majority and in such a clever way that they have been able to clothe their lawless actions with the semblance of legality.

**3.** Naturally, We do not wish that either you or the faithful should fail to receive from Us a solemn testimonial of Our gratitude for the prayers which, according to Our intention were poured forth in private and at public functions. It is most important, too, that these prayers which have been so powerful an aid to Us should be continued, and even increased, with renewed fervor. It is assuredly not in the power of man to control the course of events or of history, nor can he direct them as he may desire to the welfare of society by changing either the minds or hearts of his fellow-men. Such action, however, is well within the power of God, for He without doubt can put an end, if He so desires, to persecutions of this kind. Nor must you conclude, Venerable Brothers, that all your prayers have been in vain simply because the Mexican Government, impelled by its fanatical hatred of religion, continued to enforce more harshly and violently from day to day its unjust laws. The truth is that the clergy and the great majority of the faithful have been so strengthened in their longsuffering resistance to these laws by such an abundant shower of divine grace that they have been enabled thereby to give a glorious example of heroism. They have justly merited, too, that We, in a solemn document executed by Our Apostolic authority, should make known this fortitude to the whole Catholic world.

4. Last month on the occasion of the beatification of many martyrs of the French Revolution, spontaneously the Catholics of Mexico came to Our thoughts, for they, like those martyrs, have remained firm in their resolution to resist in all patience the unreasonable behests and commands of their persecutors rather than cut themselves off from the unity of the Church or refuse obedience to this Apostolic See. Marvelous indeed is the glory of the Divine Spouse of Christ who, through the course of the centuries, can depend, without fail, upon a brave and generous offspring ever ready to suffer prisons, stripes, and even death itself for the holy liberty of the Church!

5. It is scarcely necessary, Venerable Brothers, to go back very far in order to narrate the sad calamities which have fallen upon the Church of Mexico. It is sufficient to recall

that the frequent revolutions of modern times have ended in the majority of cases in trials for the Church and persecutions of religion. Both in 1914 and in 1915 men who seemed veritably inspired by the barbarism of former days persecuted the clergy, both secular and regular, and the sisters. They rose up against holy places and every object used in divine worship and so ferocious were they that no injury, no ignominy, no violence was too great to satisfy their persecuting mania.

6. Referring now to certain notorious facts concerning which We have already raised Our voice in solemn protest and which even the daily press recorded at great length, there is no need to take up much space in telling you of certain deplorable events which occurred even in the very recent past with reference to Our Apostolic Delegates to Mexico. Without the slightest regard for justice, for solemn promises given, or for humanity itself, one of these Apostolic Delegates was driven out of the country; another, who because of illness had left the Republic for a short time, was forbidden to return, and the third was also treated in a most unfriendly manner and forced to leave. Surely there is no one who cannot understand that such acts as these, committed against illustrious personages who were both ready and willing to bring about peace, must be construed as a great affront to their dignity as

Archbishops, to the high office which they filled, and particularly to Our authority which they represented.

7. Unquestionably the events just cited are grave and deplorable. But the examples of despotic power which We will now pass in review, Venerable Brothers, are beyond all compare, contrary to the rights of the Church, and most injurious as well to the Catholics of Mexico.

8. In the first place, let us examine the law of 1917, known as the "Political Constitution" of the federated republic of Mexico. For our present purposes it is sufficient to point out that after declaring the separation of Church and State the Constitution refuses to recognize in the Church, as if she were an individual devoid of any civil status, all her existing rights and interdicts to her the acquisition of any rights whatsoever in the future. The civil authority is given the right to interfere in matters of divine worship and in the external discipline of the Church. Priests are put on the level of professional men and of laborers but with this important difference, that they must be not only Mexicans by birth and cannot exceed a certain number specified by law, but are at the same time deprived of all civil and political rights. They are thus placed in the same class with criminals and the insane. Moreover, priests not only must inform the civil authorities but also a commission of ten citizens whenever they take possession of a church or are

transferred to another mission. The vows of religious, religious orders, and religious congregations are outlawed in Mexico. Public divine worship is forbidden unless it take place within the confines of a church and is carried on under the watchful eye of the Government. All church buildings have been declared the property of the state. Episcopal residences, diocesan offices, seminaries, religious houses, hospitals, and all charitable institutions have been taken away from the Church and handed over to the state. As a matter of fact, the Church can no longer own property of any kind. Everything that it possessed at the period when this law was passed has now become the property of the state. Every citizen, moreover, has the right to denounce before the law any person whom he thinks is holding in his own name property for the Church. All that is required in order to make such action legal is a mere presumption of guilt. Priests are not allowed by law to inherit property of any kind except it be from persons closely related to them by blood. With reference to marriage, the power of the Church is not recognized. Every marriage between Catholics is considered valid if contracted validly according to the prescriptions of the civil code.

9. Education has been declared free, but with these important restrictions: both priests and religious are forbidden to open or to conduct elementary schools. It is

not permitted to teach children their religion even in a private school. Diplomas or degrees conferred by private schools under control of the Church possess no legal value and are not recognized by the state. Certainly, Venerable Brothers, the men who originated, approved, and gave their sanction to such a law either are totally ignorant of what rights pertain *jure divino* to the Church as a perfect society, established as the ordinary means of salvation for mankind by Jesus Christ, Our Redeemer and King, to which He gave the full liberty of fulfilling her mission on earth (such ignorance seems incredible today after twenty centuries of Christianity and especially in a Catholic nation and among men who have been baptized, unless in their pride and foolishness they believe themselves able to undermine and destroy the "House of the Lord which has been solidly constructed and strongly built on the living rock") or they have been motivated by an insane hatred to attempt anything within their power in order to harm the Church. How was it possible for the Archbishops and Bishops of Mexico to remain silent in the face of such odious laws?

**10.** Immediately after their publication the hierarchy of Mexico protested in kind but firm terms against these laws, protests which Our Immediate Predecessor ratified, which were approved as well by the whole hierarchies of other countries, as well as by a great majority of individual bishops from all over the world, and which finally were confirmed even by Us in a letter of consolation of the date of the second of February, 1926, which We addressed to the Bishops of Mexico. The Bishops hoped that those in charge of the Government, after the first outburst of hatred, would have appreciated the damage and danger which would accrue to the vast majority of the people from the enforcement of those articles of the Constitution restrictive of the liberty of the Church and that, therefore, out of a desire to preserve peace they would not insist on enforcing these articles to the letter, or would enforce them only up to a certain point, thus leaving open the possibility of a modus vivendi, at least for the time being.

**11.** In spite of the extreme patience exhibited in these circumstances by both the clergy and laity, an attitude which was the result of the Bishops' exhorting them to moderation in all things, every hope of a return to peace and tranquility was dissipated, and this as a direct result of the law promulgated by the President of the Republic on the second of July, 1926, by virtue of which practically no liberty at all was left the Church. As a matter of fact, the Church was barely allowed to exist. The exercise of the sacred ministry was hedged about by the severest penalties as if it were a crime worthy of capital punishment. It is difficult, Venerable Brothers, to express in language how such perversion of civil authority grieves

Us. For whosoever reveres, as all must, God the Creator and Our Beloved Redeemer, whosoever will obey the laws of Holy Mother Church, such a man, We repeat, such a man is looked on as a malefactor, as guilty of a crime; such a man is considered fit only to be deprived of all civil rights; such a man can be thrown into prison along with other criminals. With what justice can We apply to the authors of these enormities the words which Jesus Christ spoke to the leaders of the Jews: "This is your hour, and the power of darkness." (*Luke* xxii, 53)

12. The most recent law which has been promulgated as merely an interpretation of the Constitution is as a matter of fact much worse than the original law itself and makes the enforcement of the Constitution much more severe, if not almost intolerable. The President of the Republic and the members of his ministry have insisted with such ferocity on the enforcement of these laws that they do not permit the governors of the different states of the Confederation, the civil authorities, or the military commanders to mitigate in the least the rigors of the persecution of the Catholic Church. Insult, too, is added to persecution. Wicked men have tried to place the Church in a bad light before the people; some, for example, uttering the most brazen lies in public assemblies. But when a Catholic tries to answer them, he is prevented from speaking by catcalls and personal insults hurled at his

head. Others use hostile newspapers in order to obscure the truth and to malign "Catholic Action."

13. If, at the beginning of the persecution, Catholics were able to make a defense of their religion in the public press by means of articles which made clear the truth and answered the lies and errors of their enemies, it is now no longer permitted these citizens, who love their country just as much as other citizens do, to raise their voices in protest. As a matter of fact, they are not even allowed to express their sorrow over the injuries done to the Faith of their fathers and to the liberty of divine worship. We, however, moved profoundly as We are by the consciousness of the duties imposed upon Us by our Apostolic office, will cry out to heaven, Venerable Brothers, so that the whole Catholic world may hear from the lips of the Common Father of all the story of the insane tyranny of the enemies of the Church, on the one hand, and on the other that of the heroic virtue and constancy of the bishops, priests, religious congregations, and laity ot Mexico.

14. All foreign priests and religious men have been expelled from the country. Schools for the religious education of boys and girls have been closed, either because they are known publicly under a religious name or because they happen to possess a statue or some other

religious object. Many seminaries likewise, schools, insane asylums, convents, institutions connected with churches have been closed. In practically all the states of the Republic the number of priests who may exercise the sacred ministry has been limited and fixed at the barest minimum. Even these latter are not allowed to exercise their sacred office unless they have beforehand registered with the civil authorities and have obtained permission from them so to function. In certain sections of the country restrictions have been placed on the ministry of priests which, if they were not so sad, would be laughable in the extreme. For example, certain regulations demand that priests must be of an age fixed by law, that they must be civilly married, and they are not allowed to baptize except with flowing water. In one of the states of the Confederation it has been decreed that only one bishop is permitted to live within the territory of said state, by reason of which law two other bishops were constrained to exile themselves from their dioceses. Moreover, because of circumstances imposed upon them by law, some bishops have had to leave their diocese, others have been forced to appear before the courts, several were arrested, and practically all the others live from day to day in imminent danger of being arrested.

**15.** Again, every Mexican citizen who is engaged in the education of children or of youth, or holds any public office whatsoever, has been ordered to make known publicly whether he accepts the policies of the President and approves of the war which is now being waged on the Catholic Church. The majority of these same individuals were forced, under threat of losing their positions, to take part, together with the army and laboring men, in a parade sponsored by the Regional Confederation of the Workingmen of Mexico, a socialist organization. This parade took place in Mexico City and in other towns of the Republic on the same day. It was followed by impious speeches to the populace. The whole procedure was organized to obtain, by means of these public outcries and the applause of those who took part in it, and by heaping all kinds of abuse on the Church, popular approval of the acts of the President.

**16.** But the cruel exercise of arbitrary power on the part of the enemies of the Church has not stopped at these acts. Both men and women who defended the rights of the Church and the cause of religion, either in speeches or by distributing leaflets and pamphlets, were hurried before the courts and sent to prison. Again, whole colleges of canons were rushed off to jail, the aged being carried there in their beds. Priests and laymen have been cruelly put to death in the very streets or in the public squares which front the churches. May God grant that the responsible authors of so many grave crimes return soon to their better selves and throw themselves in sorrow and with true contrition on the divine mercy; We are convinced that this is the noble revenge on their murderers which Our children who have been so unjustly put to death are now asking from God.

17. We think it well at this point, Venerable Brothers, to review for you in a few words how the bishops, priests, and faithful of Mexico have organized resistance and "set up a wall for the House of Israel, to stand in battle." (*Ezech.* xiii, 5)

18. There cannot be the slightest doubt of the fact that the Mexican hierarchy have unitedly used every means within their power to defend the liberty and good name of the Church. In the first place, they indited a joint pastoral letter to their people in which they proved beyond cavil that the clergy had always acted toward the rulers of the Republic motivated by a love for peace, with prudence and in all patience; that they had even suffered, in a spirit of almost too much tolerance, laws which were unjust; they admonished the faithful, outlining the divine constitution of the Church, that they, too, must always persevere in their religion, in such a way that they shall "obey God rather than men" (*Acts* v, 19) on every occasion when anyone tries to impose on them laws which are no less contrary to the very idea of law and do not merit the name

of law, as they are inimical to the constitution and existence itself of the Church.

**19.** When the President of the Republic had promulgated his untimely and unjust decree of interpretation of the Constitution, by means of another joint pastoral letter the Bishops protested and pointed out that to accept such a law was nothing less than to desert the Church and hand her over a slave to the civil authorities. Even if this had been done, it was apparent to all that such an act would neither satisfy her persecutors nor stop them in the pursuit of their nefarious intentions. The Bishops in such circumstances preferred to put an end to public religious functions. Therefore, they ordered the complete suspension of every act of public worship which cannot take place without the presence of the clergy, in all the churches of their diocese, beginning the last day of July, on which day the law in question went into effect. Moreover, since the civil authorities had ordered that all the churches must be turned over to the care of laymen, chosen by the mayors of the different municipalities, and could not be held in any manner whatsoever by those who were named or designated for such an office by the bishops or priests, which act transferred the possessions of the churches from the ecclesiastical authority to that of the state, the Bishops practically everywhere interdicted the faithful from accepting a place on such committees bestowed on them by the Government and even from entering a church which was no longer under the control of the Church. In some dioceses, due to difference of time and place, other arrangements were made.

**20.** In spite of all this, do not think, Venerable Brothers, that the Mexican hierarchy lost any opportunity or occasion by means of which they might do their part in calming popular feelings and bringing about concord despite the fact that they distrusted, or it would be better perhaps to say despaired of, a happy outcome to all these troubles. It is sufficient to recall in this context that the Bishops of Mexico City, who act in the capacity of procurators for their colleagues, wrote a very courteous and respectful letter to the President of the Republic in the interests of the Bishops of Huejutla, who had been arrested in a most outrageous manner and with a great display of armed force, and had been ordered taken to the city of Pachuca. The President replied to this letter by means of a hateful angry screed, a fact now become notorious. Again, when it happened that certain personages, lovers of peace, had spontaneously intervened so as to bring about a conversation between the President and the Archbishop of Morelia and the Bishop of Tabasco, the parties in question talked together for a long time and on many subjects, but with no results. Again, the Bishops debated whether they should ask the House of Representatives for the abrogation of those laws which were against the rights of the Church or if they should continue, as before, their so-called passive resistance to these laws. As a matter of fact, there existed many good reasons which seemed to them to render useless the presentation of such a petition to Congress. However, they did present the petition, which was written by Catholics quite capable of doing so because of their knowledge of law, every word of which was, moreover, weighed by the Bishops themselves with the utmost care. To this petition of the hierarchy there was added, due to the zealous efforts of the members of the Federation for the Defense of Religious Liberty, about which organization We shall have something to say later on in this letter, a great number of signatures of citizens, both men and women.

**21.** The Bishops had not been wrong in their anticipations of what would take place. Congress rejected the proposed petition almost unanimously, only one voting in favor of it, and the reason they alleged for this act was that the Bishops had been deprived of juridical personality, since they had already appealed in this matter to the Pope and therefore they had proven themselves unwilling to acknowledge the laws of Mexico. Such being the facts, what remained for the Bishops to do if not to decide that, until these unjust laws had been repealed, neither they nor the faithful would change in the slightest the policy which they had adopted? The civil authorities of Mexico, abusing both their power and the really remarkable patience of the people, are now in a position to menace the clergy and the Mexican people with even more severe punishments than those already inflicted. But how are we to overcome and conquer men of this type who are committed to the use of every type of infamy, unless we are willing, as they insist, to conclude an agreement with them which cannot but injure the sacred cause of the liberty of the Church?

22. The clergy have imitated the truly wonderful example of constancy given them by the Bishops and have themselves in turn given no less brilliant an example of fortitude through all the tedious changes of the great conflict. This example of extraordinary virtue on their part has been a great comfort to Us. We have made it known to the whole Catholic world and We praise them because "they are worthy." (*Apoc.* iii, 4) And in this special context, when We recall that every imaginable artifice was employed, that all the power and vexatious tactics of our adversaries had but one purpose, to alienate both the clergy and people from their allegiance to the hierarchy and to this Apostolic See, and that despite all this only one or two priests, from among the four thousand, betrayed in a shameful manner their holy office, it certainly seems to Us that there is nothing which We cannot hope for from the Mexican clergy.

**23.** As a matter of fact, We behold these priests standing shoulder to shoulder, obedient and respectful to the commands of their prelates despite the fact that to obey means in the majority of cases serious dangers for themselves, for they must live from their holy office, and since they are poor and do not themselves possess anything and the Church cannot support them, they are obliged to live bravely in poverty and in misery; they must say Mass in private; they must do all within their power to provide for the spiritual needs of their flocks, to keep alive and increase the flame of piety in those round about them; moreover, by their example, counsels and exhortations, they must lift the thoughts of their fellow citizens to the highest ideals and strengthen their wills so that they, too, will persevere in their passive resistance. Is it any wonder, then, that the wrath and blind hatred of our enemies are directed principally and before all else against the priesthood? The clergy, on their side, have not hesitated to go to prison when ordered, and even to face death itself with serenity and courage. We have heard recently of something which surpasses anything as yet perpetrated under the guise of these wicked laws, and which, as a matter of fact, sounds the very depths of wickedness, for We have learned that certain priests were suddenly set upon while celebrating Mass in their own homes or in the homes of friends, that the Blessed Eucharist was outraged in the basest manner, and the priests themselves carried off to prison.

24. Nor can We praise enough the courageous faithful of Mexico who have understood only too well how important it is for them that a Catholic nation in matters so serious and holy as the worship of God, the liberty of the Church, and the eternal salvation of souls should not depend upon the arbitrary will and audacious acts of a few men, but should be governed under the mercy of God only by laws which are just, which are conformable to natural, divine, and ecclesiastical law.

25. A word of very special praise is due those Catholic organizations, which during all these trying times have stood like soldiers side to side with the clergy. The members of these organizations, to the limit of their power, not only have made provisions to maintain and assist their clergy financially, they also watch over and take care of the churches, teach catechism to the children, and like sentinels stand guard to warn the clergy when their ministrations are needed so that no one may be deprived of the help of the priest. What We have just written is true of all these organizations. We wish, however, to say a word in particular about the principal organizations, so that each may know that it is highly ap proved and even praised by the Vicar of Jesus Christ.

**26.** First of all We mention the Knights of Columbus, an organization which is found in all the states of the Republic and which fortunately is made up of active and industrious members who, because of their practical lives and open profession of the Faith, as well as by their zeal in assisting the Church, have brought great honor upon themselves. This organization promotes two types of activities which are needed now more than ever. In the first place, the National Sodality of Fathers of Families, the program of which is to give a Catholic education to their own children, to protect the rights of Christian parents with regard to education, and in cases where children attend the public schools to provide for them a sound and complete training in their religion. Secondly, the Federation for the Defense of Religious Liberty, which was recently organized when it became clear as the noonday sun that the Church was menaced by a veritable ocean of troubles. This Federation soon spread to all parts of the Republic. Its members attempted, working in harmony and with assiduity, to organize and instruct Catholics so that they would be able to present a united invincible front to the enemy.

**27.** No less deserving of the Church and the fatherland as the Knights of Columbus have been and still are, We mention two other organizations, each of which has, following its own program, a special relation to what is known as "Catholic Social Action." One is the Catholic Society of Mexican Youth, and the other, the Union of Catholic Women of Mexico. These two sodalities, over and above the work which is special to each of them, promote and do all they can to have others promote the activities of the above-mentioned Federation for the Defense of Religious Liberty. Without going into details about their work, with pleasure We desire to call to your attention, Venerable Brothers, but a single fact, namely, that all the members of these organizations, both men and women, are so brave that, instead of fleeing danger, they go out in search of it, and even rejoice when it falls to their share to suffer persecution from the enemies of the Church. What a beautiful spectacle this, that is thus given to the world, to angels, and to men! How worthy of eternal praise are such deeds! As a matter of fact, as We have pointed out above, many individuals, members either of the Knights of Columbus, or officers of the Federation, of the Union of Catholic Women of Mexico, or of the Society of Mexican Youth, have been taken to prison handcuffed, through the public streets, surrounded by armed soldiers, locked up in foul jails, harshly treated, and punished with prison sentences or fines. Moreover, Venerable Brothers, and in narrating this We can scarcely keep back Our tears, some of these young men and boys have gladly met death, the rosary in their hands and the name of Christ King on their lips. Young girls, too, who were imprisoned, were criminally outraged, and these acts were deliberately made public in order to intimidate other young women and to cause them the more easily to fail in their duty toward the Church.

**28.** No one, surely, Venerable Brothers, can hazard a prediction or foresee in imagination the hour when the good God will bring to an end such calamities. We do know this much: The day will come when the Church of Mexico will have respite from this veritable tempest of hatred, for the reason that, according to the words of God "there is no wisdom, there is no prudence, there is no counsel against the Lord" (*Prov.* xxi, 30) and "the gates of hell shall not prevail" (*Matt.* xvi, 18) against the Spotless Bride of Christ.

**29.** The Church which, from the day of Pentecost, has been destined here below to a never-ending life, which went forth from the upper chamber into the world endowed with the gifts and inspirations of the Holy Spirit, what has been her mission during the last twenty centuries and in every country of the world if not, after the example of her Divine Founder, "to go about doing good"? (*Acts* x, 38) Certainly this work of the Church should have gained for her the love of all men; unfortunately the very contrary has happened as her Divine Master Himself predicted (*Matt.* x,

17, 25) would be the case. At times the bark of Peter, favored by the winds, goes happily forward; at other times it appears to be swallowed up by the waves and on the point of being lost. Has not this ship always aboard the Divine Pilot who knows when to calm the angry waves and the winds? And who is it but Christ Himself Who alone is all-powerful, who brings it about that every persecution which is launched against the faithful should react to the lasting benefit of the Church? As St. Hilary writes, "it is a prerogative of the Church that she is the vanquisher when she is persecuted, that she captures our intellects when her doctrines are questioned, that she conquers all at the very moment when she is abandoned by all." (St. Hilary of Poitiers *De Trinitate*, Bk. VII, No. 4)

30. If those men who now in Mexico persecute their brothers and fellow citizens for no other reason than that these latter are guilty of keeping the laws of God, would only recall to memory and consider dispassionately the vicissitudes of their country as history reveals them to us, they must recognize and publicly confess that whatever there is of progress, of civilization, of the good and the beautiful, in their country is due solely to the Catholic Church. In fact every man knows that after the introduction of Christianity into Mexico, the priests and religious especially, who are now being persecuted with such cruelty by an ungrateful government, worked

without rest and despite all the obstacles placed in their way, on the one hand by the colonists who were moved by greed for gold and on the other by the natives who were still barbarians, to promote greatly in those vast regions both the splendor of the worship of God and the benefits of the Catholic religion, works and institutions of charity, schools and colleges for the education of the people and their instruction in letters, the sciences, both sacred and profane, in the arts and the crafts.

31. One thing more remains for Us to do, Venerable Brothers, namely, to pray and implore Our Lady of Guadalupe, heavenly patroness of the Mexican people, that she pardon all these injuries and especially those which have been committed against her, that she ask of God that peace and concord may return to her people. And if, in the hidden designs of God that day which We so greatly desire is far distant, may she in the meantime console her faithful children of Mexico and strengthen them in their resolve to maintain their liberty by the profession of their Faith.

32. In the meanwhile, as an augury of the grace of God and as proof of Our fatherly love, We bestow from Our heart on you, Venerable Brothers, and especially on those bishops who rule the Church of Mexico, on all your clergy and your people, the Apostolic Blessing.

*Given at Rome, at St. Peter's, on the eighteenth day of November, in the year 1926, the fifth of Our Pontificate.*

## POPE PIUS XI

H.H. Pope Pius XI

# *ACERBA ANIMI*

## ENCYCLICAL OF POPE PIUS XI ON PERSECUTION OF THE CHURCH IN MEXICO TO OUR VENERABLE BROTHERS OF MEXICO, THE ARCHBISHOPS, BISHOPS, AND ORDINARIES IN PEACE AND COMMUNION WITH THE APOSTOLIC SEE.

Health, Venerable Brethren, and the Apostolic Blessing.

The concern and sorrow which We feel at the present sad plight of human society at large in no way lessen Our special solicitude for Our beloved sons of the Mexican nation and for you, Venerable Brethren, who are the more deserving of Our paternal regard because you have been so long harassed by grievous persecutions.

2. From the beginning of Our Pontificate, following the example of Our Venerable Predecessor, We endeavoured with all Our might to ward off the application of those constitutional statutes which the Holy See had several times been obliged to condemn as seriously derogatory to the most elementary and inalienable rights of the Church and of the faithful. With this intent We provided that Our Representative should take up his residence in your Republic.

3. But whereas other Governments in recent times have been eager to renew agreements with the Holy See, that of Mexico frustrated every attempt to arrive at an understanding. On the contrary, it most unexpectedly broke the promises made to Us shortly before in writing, banishing repeatedly Our Representatives and showing thereby its animosity against the Church. Thus a most rigorous application was given to Article 130 of the Constitution, against which, on account of its extreme hostility to the Church, as may be seen from Our Encyclical Iniquis afflictisque of November 18, 1926, the Holy See had to protest in the most solemn manner. Heavy penalties were then enacted against the transgressors of this deplorable article; and, as a fresh affront to the Hierarchy of the Church, it was provided that every State of the Confederation should determine the number of priests empowered to exercise the sacred ministry, in public or in private.

4. In view of these unjust and intolerant injunctions, which would have subjected the Church in Mexico to the despotism of the State and of the Government hostile to the Catholic religion, you determined, Venerable Brethren, to suspend public worship, and at the same time called on the faithful to make efficacious protest against the unjust procedure of the Government. For your apostolic firmness, you were nearly all exiled from the Republic, and from the

land of your banishment you had to witness the struggles and martyrdom of your priests and of your flock; whilst those very few amongst you who almost by miracle were able to remain in hiding in their own dioceses succeeded in effectively encouraging the faithful with the splendid example of their own undaunted spirit. Of these events We took occasion to speak in solemn allocutions, in public discourses, and more at length in the above-mentioned Encyclical Iniquis afflictisque, and We were comforted by the world's admiration for the courage displayed by the clergy in administering the Sacraments to the faithful, amid a thousand dangers and at the risk of their lives, and for the like heroism of many of the faithful, who at the cost of unheard-of sufferings and enormous sacrifices, gave valiant assistance to their priests.

5. Meanwhile We did not forbear to encourage with word and counsel the lawful Christian resistance of the priests and the faithful, exhorting them to placate by penance and prayer God's Justice, that in His merciful Providence He might shorten the time of trial. At the same time We invited Our sons throughout the world to unite their prayers to Ours in behalf of their brethren in Mexico; and wonderful were the ardour and whole-heartedness with which they responded to Our appeal. Nor did We neglect to have recourse besides to the human means at Our disposal, in order to give assistance to Our beloved sons.

Whilst addressing Our appeal to the Catholic world to give help, and generous alms, to their persecuted Mexican brethren, We urged the Governments with whom We have diplomatic relations to take to heart the abnormal and grievous condition of so many of the faithful.

6. In the face of the firm and generous resistance of the oppressed, the Government now began to give indications in various ways that it would not be averse to coming to an agreement, if only to put an end to a condition of affairs which it could not turn to its own advantage. Whereupon, though taught by painful experiences to put scant trust in such promises, We felt obliged to ask Ourselves whether it was for the good of souls to prolong the suspension of public worship. That suspension had indeed been an effective protest against the arbitrary interference of the Government; nevertheless, its continuation might have seriously prejudiced civil and religious order. Of even greater weight was the consideration that this suspension, according to grave reports which We received from various and unexceptionable sources, was productive of serious harm to the faithful. As these were bereft of spiritual helps necessary for the Christian life, and not infrequently were obliged to omit their religious duties, they ran the risk of first remaining apart from and then of being entirely separated from the priesthood, and in consequence from the very sources of supernatural life. To

this must be added the fact that the prolonged absence of almost all the Bishops from their dioceses could not fail to bring about a relaxation of ecclesiastical discipline, especially in times of such great tribulation for the Mexican Church, when clergy and people had particular need of the guidance of those "whom the Holy Ghost has placed to rule the Church of God."

7. When, therefore, in 1929 the Supreme Magistrate of Mexico publicly declared that the Government, by applying the laws in question, had no intention of destroying the "identity of the Church" or of ignoring the Ecclesiastical Hierarchy, We thought it best, having no other intention but the good of souls, to profit by the occasion, which seemed to offer a possibility of having the rights of the Hierarchy duly recognized. Seeing, therefore, some hope of remedying greater evils, and judging that the principal motives that had induced the Episcopate to suspend public worship no longer existed, We asked Ourselves whether it were not advisable to order its resumption. In this there was certainly no intention of accepting the Mexican regulations of worship, nor of withdrawing Our protests against these regulations, much less of ceasing to combat them. It was merely a question of abandoning, in view of the Government's new declarations, one of the methods of resistance, before it

could bring harm to the faithful, and of having recourse instead to others deemed more opportune.

8. Unfortunately, as all know, Our wishes and desires were not followed by the peace and favourable settlement for which We had hoped. On the contrary, to Bishops, priests, and faithful Catholics continued to be penalized and imprisoned, contrary to the spirit in which the modus vivendihad been established. To Our great distress We saw that not merely were all the Bishops not recalled from exile, but that others were expelled without even the semblance of legality. In several dioceses neither churches nor seminaries, Bishops' residences, nor other sacred edifices, were restored; notwithstanding explicit promises, priests and laymen who had steadfastly defended the faith were abandoned to the cruel vengeance of their adversaries. Furthermore, as soon as the suspension of public worship had been revoked, increased violence was noticed in the campaign of the press against the clergy, the Church, and God Himself; and it is well known that the Holy See had to condemn one of these publications, which in its sacrilegious immorality and acknowledged purpose of anti-religious and slanderous propaganda had exceeded all bounds.

9. Add to this that not only is religious instruction forbidden in the primary schools, but not infrequently

attempts are made to induce those whose duty it is to educate the future generations, to become purveyors of irreligious and immoral teachings, thus obliging the parents to make heavy sacrifices in order to safeguard the innocence of their children. We bless with all Our heart these Christian parents and all the good teachers who help them, and We urge upon you, Venerable Brethren, upon the clergy secular and regular, and upon all the faithful, the necessity of giving their utmost attention to the question of education and the formation of the young, especially among the poorer classes, since they are more exposed to atheist, masonic, and communistic propaganda, persuading yourselves that your country will be such as you build it up in the children.

10. An effort has been made to strike the Church in a still more vital spot; namely, in the existence of the clergy and the Catholic hierarchy, by trying to eliminate it gradually from the Republic. Thus the Mexican Constitution, as We have several times deplored, while proclaiming liberty of thought and conscience, prescribes with the most evident contradiction that each State of the Federal Republic must determine the number of priests to whom the exercise of the sacred ministry is allowed, not only in public churches, but even within private dwellings. This enormity is further aggravated by the way in which the law is applied. The Constitution lays down that the number of priests must be

determined, but ordains that this determination must correspond to the religious needs of the faithful and of the locality. It does not prescribe that the Ecclesiastical Hierarchy is to be ignored in this matter, and this point was explicitly recognized in the declarations of the modus vivendi. Now in the State of Michoacan one priest was assigned for every 33,000 of the faithful, in the State of Chiapas one for every 60,000, while in the State of Vera Cruz only one priest was assigned to exercise the sacred ministry for every 100,000 of the inhabitants. Everyone can see whether it is possible with such restrictions to administer the Sacraments to so many people, scattered for the most part over a vast territory. Indeed, the persecutors, as though sorry for having been too liberal and indulgent, have imposed further limitations. Some Governors closed seminaries, confiscated canonries, and determined the sacred buildings and the territory to which the ministry of the approved priest would be restricted.

11. The clearest manifestation of the will to destroy the Catholic Church itself is, however, the explicit declaration, published in some States, that the civil Authority, in granting the license for priestly ministry, recognizes no Hierarchy; on the contrary, it positively excludes from the possibility of exercising the sacred ministry all of hierarchic rank - namely, all Bishops and even those who have held the office of Apostolic Delegates.

12. We wished briefly to rehearse the salient points in the grievous condition of the Church in Mexico, so that all lovers of order and peace among nations, on seeing that such an unheard of persecution differs but little, especially in certain States, from the one raging within the unhappy borders of Russia, may from this iniquitous similarity of purpose conceive fresh ardour to stem the torrent which is subverting all social order. At the same time it is Our intention to give a new proof to you, Venerable Brethren, and to all Our beloved sons of Mexico, of the paternal solicitude with which We follow you in your tribulation: the same solicitude that inspired the instructions which We gave you last January through Our Beloved Son the Cardinal Secretary of State, and which was communicated to you by Our Apostolic Delegate. In matters strictly connected with religion, it is undoubtedly Our duty and Our right to establish the reasons and norms that all who glory in the name of Catholics are under the obligation of obeying. In this connection We are anxious to recall to mind that when We issued these instructions We gave due consideration to all the reports and advices that came to Us either from the Hierarchy or the faithful. We say all, even those that appeared to counsel a return to a severer line of conduct, with the total suspension of public worship throughout the Republic, as in 1926.

13. Concerning, therefore the conduct to follow, since the number of priests is not equally limited in every State, nor the rights of the Ecclesiastical Hierarchy everywhere equally disregarded, it is evident that, according to the different application of the unhappy decrees, different likewise must be the conduct of the Church and the Catholics. Here it seems just to pay a special tribute of praise to those Mexican Bishops who, according to advices received, have wisely interpreted the instructions We have inculcated time and again. To this We wish to call attention; for if some persons, urged rather by zeal for the defense of their own faith than by the prudence so necessary in delicate situations, may from diverse conduct in diverse circumstances have imagined contradictory judgments on the part of the Bishops, let them now be certain that such an accusation is utterly unfounded. Nevertheless, since any restriction whatever of the number of priests is a grave violation of divine rights, it will be necessary for the Bishops, the clergy, and the Catholic laity to continue to protest with all their energy against such violation, using every legitimate means. For even if these protests have no effect on those who govern the country, they will be effective in persuading the faithful, especially the uneducated, that by such action the State attacks the liberty of the Church, which liberty the Church can never renounce, no matter what may be the violence of the persecutors.

14. And therefore, just as We have read with satisfaction the protests recently made by the Bishops and priests of the diocese that are victims of the deplorable measures of the Government, so We join Our protests to yours before the whole world, and in a special manner before the Rulers of the Nations, to make them realize that the persecution of Mexico, besides being an outrage against God, against His Church, and against the conscience of a Catholic people, is also an incentive to the subversion of the social order, which is the aim of those organizations professing to deny God.

15. Meanwhile, in order to remedy to some extent the calamitous conditions that afflict the Church in Mexico, We must avail ourselves of those means which We still have in hand, so that, by the maintenance of divine worship as far as possible in every place, the light of faith and the sacred fire of charity may not be extinguished among those unhappy populations. Certainly, the laws are iniquitous that are impious, as We have already said, and condemned by God for everything that they iniquitously and impiously derogate from the rights of God and of the Church in the government of souls. Nevertheless, it would be a vain and unfounded fear to think that one is cooperating with these iniquitous legislative ordinances which oppress him, were he to ask the Government which imposes these things for permission to carry out public

worship, and hence to hold that it is one's duty to refrain absolutely from making such a request. Such an erroneous opinion and conduct might lead to a total suspension of public worship, and would, without doubt, inflict grievous harm on the entire flock of the faithful.

16. It is well to observe that to approve such an iniquitous law, or spontaneously to give to it true and proper cooperation, is undoubtedly illicit and sacrilegious. but absolutely different is the case of one who yields to such unjust regulations solely against his will and under protest, and who besides does everything he can to lessen the disastrous effects of the pernicious law. In fact, the priest finds himself compelled to ask for that permission without which it would be impossible for him to exercise his sacred ministry for the good of souls; it is an imposition to which he is forced to submit in order to avoid a greater evil. His behaviour, consequently, is not very different from that of one who having been robbed of his belongings is obliged to ask his unjust despoiler for at least the use of them.

17. In truth, the danger of formal cooperation, or of any approval whatever of the present law, is removed, as far as is necessary, by the protests energetically expressed by this Apostolic See, by the whole Episcopate and the people of Mexico. To these are added the precautions of the priest

himself, who, although already appointed to the sacred ministry by his own Bishop, is obliged to ask the Government for the possibility of holding divine service; and, far from approving the law that unjustly imposes such a request, submits to it materially, as the saying is, and only in order to remove an obstacle to the exercise of the sacred ministry: an obstacle that would lead, as We have said, to a total cessation of worship, and hence to exceedingly great harm to innumerable souls. In much the same manner the faithful and the sacred ministers of the early Church, as history relates, sought permission, by means of gifts even, to visit and comfort the martyrs detained in prison and to administer the Sacraments to them; yet surely no one could have thought that by so doing they in some way approved or justified the conduct of the persecutors.

18. Such is the certain and safe doctrine of the Church. If, however, the putting of it into practice should cause scandal to some of the faithful, it will be your duty, Venerable Brethren, to enlighten them carefully and exactly. If, after you have performed this office of explanation and persuasion, according to these Our directions, anyone should cling stubbornly to his own false opinion, let him know that he can hardly escape the reproach of disobedience and obstinacy.

19. Let all, then, continue in that unity of purpose and obedience that We have praised in the clergy, on another occasion, at length and with lively satisfaction. And, putting aside all uncertainties and fears easily understood in the first moments of the persecution, let the priests with their proved spirit of abnegation render ever more intense their sacred ministry, particularly among the young and the common people, striving to carry on a work of persuasion and of charity especially among the enemies of the Church, who combat her because they do not know her.

20. And here We recommend anew a point that We have greatly at heart, namely, the necessity of instituting and furthering to an ever greater extent Catholic Action, according to the directions communicated at Our command by Our Apostolic Delegate. This is undoubtedly a difficult undertaking in its first stages, and especially in the present circumstances - an undertaking slow at times in producing the desired effects, but necessary and much more efficacious than any other means, as is abundantly proved by the experience of every nation that has been tried in the crucible of religious persecution.

21. To Our beloved Mexican sons We recommend with all Our heart the closest union with the Church and the Hierarchy, manifesting it by their docility to her teachings

and directions. Let them not neglect to have recourse to the Sacraments, sources of grace and strength; let them instruct themselves in the truths of religion; let them implore mercy from God on their unhappy nation, and let them make it both a duty and an honour to cooperate with the apostolate of the priesthood in the ranks of Catholic Action.

22. We wish to pay a special tribute of praise to those members of the clergy, secular and regular, and of the Catholic laity, who, moved by burning zeal for religion and maintaining themselves in close obedience to this Apostolic See, have written glorious pages in the recent history of the Church in Mexico. At the same time We exhort them earnestly in the Lord to continue to defend the sacred rights of the Church with that generous abnegation of which they have given such a splendid example, always following the norms laid down by this Apostolic See.

23. We cannot conclude without turning in a very special manner to you, Venerable Brethren, who are the faithful interpreters of Our thoughts. We wish to tell you that We feel all the more closely united to you, in proportion to the hardships you are meeting with in your apostolic ministry. We are certain that, being so close to the heart of the Vicar of Christ, you will draw comfort and strength from this knowledge to persevere in the holy and arduous enterprise

of leading to salvation the flock entrusted to you. And that the grace of God may ever assist you and His Mercy support you, with all paternal affection, We impart to you and to Our beloved sons so sorely tried, the Apostolic Benediction.

*Given at Rome, at Saint Peter's, on the feast of the Dedication of Saint Michael the Archangel, the twenty-ninth day of September in the year 1932, the eleventh of Our Pontificate.*

**POPE PIUS XI**

A clandestine Mass in Mexico during the Cristiada

# BIBLIOGRAPHY

Bailey, David C. *Viva Cristo Rey! The Cristero Rebellion and the Church-State Conflict in Mexico*. University of Texas Press. Austin, Texas. 1974.

Dragon, Antonio, S.J.,. *Vida Intima del Padre Pro. Obra Nacional de la Buena Prensa*. Mexico City. 2005

Facius, Antonio Ruiz. *México Cristero*. Asociación Pro-Cultura Occidental, A.C. Guadalajara, Jalisco – Mexico. 1960

Hanley, O.F.M., Boniface. *No Strangers to Violence, No Strangers to Love*. Ave Maria Press. Notre Dame, Indiana. 1983

Norman, Mrs. George. *God's Jester: The Story of Fr. Michael Pro, S.J.* Benzinger Brothers, Inc. New York. 1930

Parsons, S.J., Fr. Wilfrid. *Mexian Martyrdom* – Tan Books and Publishers, Inc. Rockford, Illinois. 1987

Tuck, Jim. *The Holy War in Los Altos*, Tucson, Arizona. University of Arizona. 1982

Meyer, Jean. *La Cristiada* (3 Volumes), Siglo Veintiuno Editores Mexico City. 1974

www.vatican.va

# Now You Can Experience the Powerful True Story of the Cristeros - LIVE!

Bring Cristero expert and author of *For Greater Glory: The Cristero War and Mexico's Struggle for Religious Freedom* to speak to your parish or group.

A respected speaker, Mr. Quezada has presented his inspiring and informative presentations to international audiences of all ages in both English and Spanish for many years.

To invite Ruben Quezada to your event call 1.800.526.2151 or visit: **www.saintjoe.com/testimonials.asp**

Author **Ruben Quezada** is Director of Operations for the **Catholic Resource Center** and **Saint Joseph Communications, Inc.** in Southern California.

---

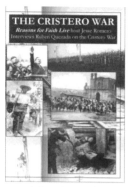

*As heard on EWTN Global Catholic Radio!*

# FREE MP3 Download with Ruben Quezada and Jesse Romero

Jesse Romero, well-known Catholic apologist and host of EWTN Radio's **Reasons for Faith LIVE,** joins author Ruben Quezada for two hour-long interviews on the history of the Cristiada. This mini-series on the Cristero War is an excellent introduction to this crucial episode in the Church's ongoing battle for religious freedom. Yours FREE when you visit **http://www.saintjoe.com/religiousfreedom.asp.**

Inspiring DVDs relating to *For Greater Glory* and the Cristero War

# ¡VIVA CRISTO REY!

Discover the true history of the Cristeros on this remarkable DVD from author and recognized Cristero expert **Ruben Quezada**. Includes many authentic images of the historical figures and events of the Cristiada.

1 DVD - $14.95 (Available in English or Spanish)

# www.vivacristorey.com

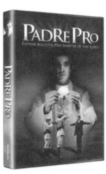

### CONVERSION TESTIMONIES

English: Eduardo Verástegui
(*For Greater Glory, Bella*)
**1 DVD - $19.95**

Spanish: Karyme Lozano
(*For Greater Glory*)
**1 DVD - $19.95**

### PADRE PRO MOVIE

Based on the admirable life of Miguel Agustin Pro, S.J. A priest dedicated to the Catholic Faith and a Martyr for Christ. (Spanish)

**1 DVD - $15.95**

Visit the website for a full list of products in English and Spanish

# FREE MP3 Download
# on Religious Freedom

Just like in Mexico during the Cristero War (depicted in the movie *For Greater Glory*) religious freedom is under attack today right here in the United States! But what can Catholic Americans do to defend against the unrelenting barrage of the "culture of death" against the Catholic Faith? The answer lies in a new FREE audio presentation:

## Overcoming the Attack on Religious Liberty

This amazing FREE download features the solidly Catholic voices of: **Father William Casey** of the Fathers of Mercy, **Jesse Romero, M.A.,** of the "Reasons for Faith LIVE" radio show, popular Catholic author and apologist **Stephen K. Ray,** and renowned conference speaker and the founder of Ignatius Press **Father Joseph Fessio, S.J.** In this powerful presentation, you and others will hear:

- Why Catholics MUST stand up for their Faith NOW more than ever - while there's still time
- Why the government doesn't "give us rights," and why rights come from God
- How to make an effective spiritual response to the attack on religious freedom
- What to pray for to end this crisis
- Why government subsidies are a "deal with the devil"
- Why "An unjust law is NO law," as the Church has taught for 2,000 years
- Why we must obey God rather than men
- What's in store for our children if we fail!

And all that is just the tip of the iceberg of what you'll discover in this hard-hitting, no-holds-barred FREE presentation. These interviews are straight talk that's straight from the heart, with nothing held back.

## Download FREE
### http://www.saintjoe.com/religiousfreedom.asp